DATE DUE		

Straight Talk About Teenage Gambling

Straight Talk About Teenage Gambling

Carol Silverman Saunders

☑® Facts On File, Inc.

Straight Talk About Teenage Gambling

Facts On File, Inc.
11 Penn Plaza
New York, NY 10001

Library of Congress Cataloging-in-Publication Data
Saunders, Carol Silverman.
    Straight talk about teenage gambling / Carol Silverman Saunders.
    p. cm.
    Includes bibliographical references (p.   ) and index.
    Summary: Explores the issue of teenage gambling, discussing its addictive nature, effects on the individual and the family, and place in society.
    ISBN 0-8160-3718-3 (alk. paper)
    1. Teenage gamblers—Juvenile literature. 2. Compulsive gambling—Juvenile literature. [1. Gambling.] I. Title.
    HV6710.S28   1999
    362.2'5—dc21   98-25719

Facts On File books are available at special discounts when purchased in bulk quantities for businesses, associations, institutions, or sales promotions. Please call our Special Sales Department in New York at (212) 967-8800 or (800) 322-8755.

You can find Facts On File on the World Wide Web at
http://www.factsonfile.com

Text design by Cathy Rincon
Cover design by Smart Graphics

Printed in the United States of America

MP FOF 10 9 8 7 6 5 4 3 2

This book is printed on acid-free paper.

Contents

Dedicated to
Bob, Lauren,
and Mitchell

Acknowledgments

Many thanks to the following people for their help, advice, and input into this book:

Ed Looney, for his insights into the lives of teen gamblers, for his wonderful school programs on gambling, and for his tireless dedication to helping people of all ages overcome compulsive gambling; Dr. Shaffer, Dr. Derevensky, and Dr. Svendsen, for contributing the excellent research on teens and gambling; Paul Doocey, for providing information on the gambling industry; Nicole Bowen and Laurie Likoff, for knowing that teens need information about gambling; and the teens and young adults who shared with me their experiences with gambling—you know who you are.

Straight Talk
About Teenage
Gambling

1

Gambling in a High-Tech World

Dave* and his friends like to play poker. Every weekend, the five of them gather at Steve's house. They play at Steve's because there's a big table in his den, perfect for playing cards.

The poker buddies have certain rituals they always follow. For example, Dave always wears his "lucky" gray T-shirt and his "lucky" baseball hat. During a game, he turns his hat upside down and uses it to hold his poker chips.

Dave has convinced the guys to limit their bets. The most any player can bet is $5 a night, and the maximum bet on a game is $1. This works for them because they can play for nearly four hours on the $5. Dave figures that he and his friends play poker for longer than a movie lasts, and it actually costs them less than the movies.

---

*Everyone identified by first name only in this book is a *composite*—a portrait drawn from details that come from many different people.

Sam likes a different form of gambling, one that is connected with his fascination with Hollywood. He wants to be a director and plans on going to film school. He sees every movie he can and rents videos every night. Sam follows the movie gossip in magazines and on television. One day he reads about how to run an Academy Awards betting pool. Sam decides his soccer team would be the perfect group to participate in such a pool.

So Sam prints up a list of the Oscar nominees in each category and passes out the photocopied sheets to his soccer teammates. His friends can bet on who will be the winner in each category—who will win best actor, best picture, and so on. Each prediction costs $1 to bet on, with a $5 limit. When the actual winners are announced on television, Sam will divide up the money according to who guessed correctly.

At first, Sam's coach doesn't think the pool is appropriate because he says it is gambling. Sam convinces him it is just for fun. Next year he thinks he may start an election pool, so his teammates can bet on which political candidates will win the next election.

Andrea never gambles at all, not even on things like Sam's awards pool. She doesn't understand why other people like to play poker for money the way Dave does, or why they buy lottery tickets or gamble in casinos. She says all gambling is like crumbling up dollar bills and throwing them in the garbage. Some of her friends try to get her to bet on football games, but she always says no. Lately, it's been getting harder to hang out with her friends and not join in the gambling. It seems that in Andrea's clique, if you are into sports, you have to gamble on them. Andrea doesn't think that gambling and sports have to go together, but her friends are really pressuring her to participate.

Mike has an intense interest in gambling, as a result of having heard his parents talk about it for years. He watched them play poker and bingo every weekend throughout his childhood. When they went to the nearby casino without him, he felt sure he was missing a lot of excitement.

Since elementary school, Mike has been flipping quarters. It was a fun way to pass time, and he never thought of it as gambling. He started buying lottery tickets in middle school. Now he bets through a bookie on football, baseball, basketball, and hockey games. He sneaks in and bets at the racetrack, and he has also started going to the casino nearby. If he wears a suit, he looks old enough to get past the security guards without being questioned. But Mike has a problem. He is in debt to his bookie for $2,000. He pawned his watch to help pay his bookie, but he only got $20 for it. Mike has even turned to crime in a desperate attempt to get money for the bookie—last week he broke into a soda machine to get quarters to play the slot machines. When he wins a big slot machine prize, then he'll be able to pay his debts and still have money left over, he reasons.

The Gambling Society

Like you, Dave, Sam, Andrea, and Mike live in a society that openly encourages legal gambling for adults. Your generation of teens is the first to grow up with such a lifestyle. Gambling has been around for thousands of years, but never to such an extent as now. Never before have people been exposed to daily advertising that depicts gambling as a worthwhile recreational activity. Almost all states have lotteries, and many have casinos and racetracks. Gambling CD-ROM games and online gambling are easy ways to gamble right from your home. Vacation destinations such as Las Vegas and Atlantic City, once geared exclusively to adults, now cater to families. Perhaps you and your family have been on vacation there or somewhere else that features gambling.

Gambling means placing a bet, whether for money or not, where the outcome of an event is uncertain or depends on chance, and in which the player may or may not be able to improve the chances of winning because of his or her skill. Placing a bet means risking a set amount of money or other object of value on the outcome of the event. Betting $10 on who will win the Super Bowl is gambling. So is betting your dessert on who wins an arm wrestling match. It does not matter whether the bet is money, food, or some other object of value.

The three most popular ways for teens to gamble are card playing with family and/or friends, sports betting on football or baseball pools (with or without illegal *bookies* —those who determine odds and pay off bets), and bets on games of personal skill such as bowling or golf.

Even though it is never legal for teens under 18 to buy lottery tickets or gamble in casinos and racetracks, many do. Often they start when introduced to it by their parents. That's what happened to Mike. It is not illegal for teens to play poker for money like Dave does or to run pools, like Sam. However, gambling experts say, legal or not, it is very easy to develop problems with these types of gambling, too. Most people who gamble limit it to a social activity, but a significant number find their gambling becomes a problem. Their lives become completely preoccupied with gambling; they are unable to cut back or control it. The number of teens developing this problem will increase with the proliferation of legalized gambling in our country.

By looking at all the facts about gambling and examining your feelings about it, you can make choices that work for *you*. You may feel that there are fun, enjoyable, and positive aspects of gambling, but you may also come to see what can be the uncomfortable, unpleasant, and even frightening aspects of this activity. This book will help you decide whether or not to gamble, how to make legal and low-risk choices if you do, and what to do if your gambling gets out of control. You will also find out how gambling may be affecting a friend or family member.

Dave has been sitting out the past few weeks' poker games. He has decided that rather than spend his money on poker, since he usually loses, he is going to save up for a concert ticket. He also wants to buy a few new CDs. The other guys are disappointed that he has decided not to play. Dave's friend Mario has started to call Dave the "poker baby." Another poker buddy, Hitash, keeps telling Dave the game is no fun without him. This annoys Dave, though he tries not to show that he feels pressured. Dave thinks that it is a personal decision whether or not to gamble, and he resents that his friends are bothering him about it. Dave misses his poker buddies, but he feels good about making a decision and sticking to it.

Sam gambles for fun, without betting large amounts of money. Because he knows a lot about the movie industry, he feels he is not taking a big risk when he bets his $5. In fact, for the past three years, before he even started the pool, Sam has correctly predicted the best actor and actress, best movie, and best screenplay. Last year, for the $5 he wagered, he won $35. This made him happy for weeks. Some of his friends, of course, lost their $5 bet. They were not very happy about it, but at least they had not lost a lot of money.

Since Andrea's friends are into gambling on sports and she isn't, she feels left out. Some of her friends have already stopped calling her, and she hasn't been invited to a game in a while. Andrea works hard, earning money shoveling snow and raking leaves in her neighborhood. She puts her earnings into a savings account at the bank because she's interested in buying a new computer. She has already bought a new bike and several video games with her earnings. Andrea can't see why she should risk losing the money she has worked so hard to earn.

Andrea is thinking perhaps she should find some new friends. There's a girl who recently transferred to her high school. Maybe Andrea will sit with her at lunch tomorrow instead of at her usual table. Perhaps, like Andrea, the new girl will be into activities other than gambling. This is taking a risk because Andrea's friends may drop her. But rather than risking money on gambling, this is the kind of risk that Andrea is willing to take.

Mike constantly thinks about when he is going to gamble again. While eating his breakfast, he thinks about whether after school he is going to be able to get to the store that sells lottery tickets. Before sleeping, he lays in bed plotting how he will play his next round of blackjack at the casino on the weekend. Unfortunately, Mike's parents don't know the extent of his problems, because they have their own serious ones. Mike's father is never at home—he's always out gambling. Mike's mother has to work two jobs to pay the bills, because Mike's father can't keep a job. They are always fighting and are thinking of getting divorced.

Sometimes, Mike feels worried and depressed about his situation. It seems he is always thinking about where to get more money. He worries about paying off his bookie. It scares him that he has considered stealing cash from his aunt's purse. When he thinks about the danger of getting caught doing that or something else illegal, he feels anxious and depressed. He wishes he could make his problems stop. But he can't imagine how.

Gambling Ancestors

People have been gambling for thousands of years. Gambling games have been identified as long ago as 3000 B.C., in the remains of the ancient Near Eastern city of Babylon.

Lotteries were held in Europe, as early as the Middle Ages (ca. 500 to 1500). The first known government-sponsored lottery was held in England under Queen Elizabeth I in 1566.

Gambling is described in famous literature. The Bible mentions "casting lots," which is a form of gambling. William Shakespeare referred to gambling in many of his plays. The Russian novelist Fyodor Dostoyevsky wrote a novel entitled *The Gambler* in 1866—to help repay *his* gambling debts.

The United States also has a long history of gambling. Early American heroes such as George Washington and Thomas Jefferson were involved in gambling. George Washington was said to gamble with cards all day when it was raining, and so did the soldiers he led. A popular game they played was called toss-up, in which one soldier called heads or tails and then threw a bunch of halfpennies in the air. When they landed, the thrower gathered the coins that showed the side he called, and the other player took the rest. Thomas Jefferson was so in debt from gambling that he planned to hold a lottery, offering his Monticello estate as the prize. He died before this could take place. During the mid-1800s, gambling was very popular with the miners and settlers of the western United States. Here is a chart of significant gambling dates in America's history:

1621: Restrictions are placed on gambling in the colonies.

1665: The first horseracing course in America is built in New York.

1682: The Quaker government of Pennsylvania prohibits gambling, but people gamble anyway.

1790: Lotteries are widely used to finance civic projects.

1815: The first casino in America opens in New Orleans, Louisiana.

1835: The government of New Orleans declares casinos to be illegal.

1887: Slot machines are invented.

1910: Legalized gambling in the United States is practically nonexistent due to anti-gambling legislation.

1931: Nevada's state government legalizes casino gambling.

1930s to 1940s: Casinos and horseracing become common in many places.

1941: Las Vegas casinos begin to be built.

1946: Famous gangster Bugsy Siegel opens a casino in Las Vegas.

1955: The U.S. Senate investigates organized crime ties to casinos.

1960s: State lotteries become common.

1978: Casinos are legalized in Atlantic City, New Jersey.

1988: The Indian Gaming Regulatory Act authorizes federal regulation of tribal casinos.

1997: Internet gambling becomes common, with more than 300 gambling sites available.

The Difference Between Risk Taking and Gambling

We are constantly compelled to make choices involving different degrees and types of risk. The level of risk that is comfortable for one person may be viewed as foolish by others. For example, taking the scenarios sketched previously, many people might risk their $5 on Sam's pool rather than take Andrea's gamble of changing seats at lunch and risk losing friends. Risk means that a decision is made to engage in an activity with an uncertain outcome. However, in the case of gambling, a decision's outcome usually has to do with winning or losing money or other material goods.

Sam's awards pool is gambling. Even though the bets are small, the outcome is uncertain. But Andrea's "wager" on changing her lunchtime seat is not gambling. Andrea is taking a risk by changing her seat, but there is no material gain or loss based on the outcome. Other examples of risks that are not bets are painting a picture and entering it in an art contest, being nice to someone who is unpopular, and buying a present for someone who you are not sure will give you one in return.

Some people say that risking money by investing in the stock market is the same as gambling. Others, however, disagree. In May 1997, the New York Stock Exchange sued a Las Vegas casino that had a Wall Street theme. The New York, New York Hotel & Casino created an entrance made to look like the stock exchange, with signs that said "New York New York Stock Exchange," "New York $lot Exchange," and "NY$E." The real New York stock exchange said that the use of its name and facade suggested that the Stock Exchange sponsored or licensed the hotel and casino, which it did not. The stock exchange argued that there are big differences between gambling and investing in the stock market. First, it said that gambling is entertainment, while the stock market is concerned with growing businesses. In addition, when you invest in the stock market, you are buying shares of ownership in a company and its future business prospects. In exchange for your money, you get a share of the company. With gambling, you are just buying a chance for a payoff. You are not getting anything tangible. However, "buying on margin" in the stock market can be considered a form of gambling because it means buying stock on credit, without necessarily having the money to back it up.

Types of Gamblers

Experts who study gambling look at how much gambling people do in order to understand how gambling affects people. The range of gambling activity can be looked at as a continuum, starting from the person who never gambles and never would, like Andrea. The opposite extreme is the person whose entire life is organized around gambling, like Mike. There are many people who fall in between these parameters, like Dave and Sam.

Non-gamblers

People with the lowest frequency of gambling are called non-gamblers by the experts. Non-gamblers have no interest in gambling. They would rather spend their time and money on other activities. Andrea, and most teens, fall into this category.

Recreational Gamblers

The next most common type of gambler is the recreational gambler, such as Dave and Sam. Recreational gamblers are also called *social* or *casual* gamblers. These people view gambling as a form of entertainment. If they lose money gambling, they just consider it to be the cost of the entertainment, in the same way they would consider the cost of admission to a movie. Consequently, they are able to monitor what they spend on gambling according to their budget. They don't feel overpowered by their desire to gamble. Just as some people occasionally go to a movie or buy a CD they can't really afford, so recreational gamblers might occasionally lose money they can not afford to lose, but they can easily manage to stop gambling until the budget is balanced again.

Serious Gamblers

Serious gamblers are next most common. These are people who gamble frequently, but seemingly without any serious consequences. Their families and jobs (or schoolwork) take priority to their gambling activities and they haven't yet fallen into debt as a result of gambling.

Problem Gamblers

Problem gamblers are serious gamblers who are in danger of becoming compulsive gamblers. They no longer have fun when they gamble. A problem gambler is always in debt, may often demonstrate irresponsible behavior, and frequently feels anxious.

Compulsive Gamblers

Compulsive gamblers are those who consider gambling the only important thing in life. *Compulsive* means a strong and irrational desire to do a particular thing. The term can apply to gambling, or drinking, or even cleanliness. Compulsive behavior is irrational, because it wastes a huge amount of time and accomplishes very little, if anything. Mike is a compulsive gambler.

Gambling affects every aspect of a compulsive gambler's life, but a compulsive gambler doesn't realize that. Compulsive gamblers will bet even if they don't have enough money, because they will borrow or steal, if necessary. They will bet even if they haven't got enough money to buy food or to pay the bills. They will bet even if their family and friends warn them that they are betting too much. Compulsive gamblers are no longer wagering for fun, because they must constantly worry about how they are going to get enough money to gamble again. Their compulsion to gamble feels too strong to ever stop. Their desire to continue is stronger than any desire to stop.

Compulsive gamblers may lose a job or fail a course because they are so preoccupied with gambling. They may lose a boyfriend or a girlfriend because so many movie dates have been broken to go to the track or watch a game that they have bet on. The compulsive gambler might even steal money from family, friends, or strangers to support the habit.

Professional Gamblers and Criminal Gamblers

There are two additional types of gamblers, but very few people are in these groups. *Professional gamblers* make a living at gambling but develop no lifestyle problems.

Criminal gamblers cheat others by using marked cards, fixed dice, and other illegal activities. These types of gamblers may also be problem or compulsive gamblers, but not necessarily.

Teen Gamblers

Many gambling experts are studying how teens fit into these categories. In April 1995, Dr. Howard J. Shaffer, associate professor and director at Harvard Medical School, Division on Addictions; Elizabeth M. George, executive director of the Minnesota Council on Compulsive Gambling, Inc.; and Thomas Cummings, executive director of the Massachusetts Council on Compulsive Gambling, organized the North American Think Tank on Youth Gambling Issues. They, along with other experts, wrote a report adding a new category to the list of types of gamblers, one that applies especially to teenagers. *Underage gamblers* is the new group they identified: people under the minimum legal age for gambling who gamble anyway.

Gambling by the Numbers

Even though gambling experts believe that thousands, perhaps millions of teens gamble, there have not yet been any national surveys to generate national statistics on this issue. With all the attention teen gambling is getting, national studies will probably be done soon. In the meantime, experts rely on local and state surveys, studies, and estimates. Here are some of the facts and figures taken from the April 1995 report of the North American Think Tank on Youth Gambling Issues:

- More than 7 million juveniles under 18 gamble, according to a compilation of independent surveys taken in New Jersey, California, Virginia, and Connecticut.

- Between 4 percent and 7 percent of these young people meet the criteria for problem gambling.
- Between 10 percent and 14 percent of the teens who gamble experience some symptoms of compulsive gambling, for a total of around 1 million teens nationally.
- Rates for compulsive gambling among those adolescents who gamble have been found to be twice as high as the rate of problems among adult gamblers.
- Young males gamble more frequently than young females.
- Students who have a parent with a gambling problem are more likely to gamble than those without.

Other Facts

- Some form of gambling is legal (for adults, never for teens) in every state but Utah and Hawaii and in every Canadian province. These forms of gambling include lotteries, racetracks, casinos, gambling on Indian reservations, and charitable games (raffles, bingo, and other games in which the proceeds go to charity).
- There are probably many more teens who gamble than show up in studies because most people don't like to admit to gambling.
- Although it is not known how much money teens spend on gambling, experts believe it is likely to be hundreds of millions of dollars.
- Even though it is illegal for anyone under age 21 to gamble in New Jersey in a casino, more than 57,000 minors were prevented from entering and 47,000 were escorted from gaming floors there in the first six months of 1995 alone, according to the *Newark Star-Ledger's* March 5, 1995 article "Gambling Fever Infecting NJ Teens."
- Between 5 to 7 percent of adults are compulsive gamblers, according to the National Council on Problem Gambling.

- States with casinos, such as New Jersey and Nevada, have higher rates of compulsive gamblers than do noncasino states, according to the National Council on Problem Gambling.
- Iowa had a rate of 1.7 percent compulsive gamblers before it legalized gambling, but after it legalized gambling, the rate jumped to 5.4 percent, according to the National Council on Problem Gambling.
- Untreated compulsive gambling costs society an average of $50,000 per gambler annually—in debt, lost productivity, legal and penal system costs, welfare, and other forms of social support for victims and their families, according to the National Council on Problem Gambling.
- Gambling is growing. Casinos hosted 15 million visits from more than 34 million households in 1995, an increase of more than 20 percent over 1994, according to *Casino Journal,* a magazine published for the casino industry.
- A record 35,000 calls were made to compulsive gambling hot lines in 1996. Twenty percent were from teens and young adults, 45 percent of whom said they bet on sports, according to the National Council on Problem Gambling.

Our Gambling Society

It's no wonder that teens like to gamble. Gambling offers excitement, risk, and competition, all of which are valued in American society. The excitement of gambling can seem like a desirable escape from everyday life. By contrast, chores, school, homework, and family life may seem dull to teens lured by the possibility of winning money through gambling.

Risking money on gambling may seem harmless compared to other risks we take. Some people might say, for example, that you can risk your life just by walking across the street. Certainly, there are many small and large risks we take every day. The results of the risks we take may be good or bad. For example, when we expose our true selves to others, we risk that our feelings may be hurt. On the other hand, our relationships might grow deeper and more satisfying. Risking a fast pitch in a baseball game might help you win the game—or lose it. Risking enrollment in a tough course might bring your grades down—or open you to new opportunities for learning new things and discovering your own potential.

Competition between gamblers may feel familiar because competition exists in all areas of life. You may compete with your brothers and sisters for the last piece of pie or the chance to choose the family vacation spot. You compete with other students for the lead in a school play, a place on the volleyball team, or for the prize in a geography contest. And of course, you compete with other athletes when you engage in sports.

Society also explicitly supports gambling in a variety of ways. Governments sponsor gambling through lotteries. Religious organizations sponsor raffles and bingo games. This government and religious organization support of gambling may give the impression that it is a wholesome activity.

In most states, you are likely to be exposed to gambling ads on television, billboards, radio, and in newspapers. All this media attention to gambling makes you think about gambling, even if on your own you wouldn't. The fact that society allows gambling advertising is yet another show of support. For this reason, some people think that lottery ads and results should not be shown on television, just as ads for cigarettes are no longer allowed on TV.

Perhaps because gambling is billed as an adult activity, many teens are intrigued by the idea. Gambling at a casino on an 18th birthday or as a post-prom activity has become a rite of passage for many teens.

Today, many casinos portray themselves as family-oriented. They offer child care for children and activities for teens. Huge volcanoes, tigers, and pirate battles make the casinos seem like an amusement park. Even though children and teens can't legally gamble at these casinos, just being there with their parents may make them want to gamble as soon as they can.

Society is currently trying to deal with the new phenomenon of gambling on the Internet. Net gambling entrepreneurs are working as fast as they can to get sites up and running before federal or state governments decide that it's illegal. However, no matter what the government decides, cybergambling will probably always be available, legal or not. This is because the Internet is probably too gigantic and too all-encompassing for any government to control.

2

Teen Gambling in the News

Sam did start an election pool, and it was very successful. He won $30—not as much as he had taken in from the Oscar pool, but not bad. He was so excited about the money he won in his two pools that he started thinking about other ways he could make money gambling. Maybe he could set up an arm wrestling match and have friends bet on the outcome, or organize a gathering to bet on a televised football game. These ideas appealed to Sam because they also involved socializing with his friends, something he really enjoyed.

Andrea knew that Tom, one of her friends who had been gambling a lot, owed a lot of money to a bookie. She heard that the bookie came to Tom's house at night. The bookie showed him a photograph of a car that was smashed with baseball bats. He said that this would happen to Tom's car and his parent's car if he didn't pay up soon. Tom told some friends the next day in school what had happened. The day after that, Tom started thinking about committing suicide. He was terrified of what his parents would do to him if they found out he owed so much money, and he felt he couldn't face their reaction. He took an overdose of pills and nearly died, but doctors were able to save him.

Mike has begun to wonder if he should try to cut back on his gambling. After all, he does owe a lot of money and he doesn't like feeling worried all the time. But when Mike tries to stop, he finds that he feels even more nervous. Just the thought of missing a chance to bet makes him feel anxious—as though he were missing the chance of a lifetime.

Besides, it's Super Bowl weekend. This is his chance to win back all the money he's lost this year and more besides. "I'll stop after this game," Mike thinks. Mike is invited to two Super Bowl parties and goes to both of them, to give him even more chances to bet on games. At one of the parties, the guys get really intense about the game because the team they're betting on is losing. One boy pushes another, and a fight starts.

These kinds of incidents happen every day but don't always get reported in the news. Teen gamblers make mistakes, commit crimes, and even take their own lives. Some of their stories do make it to the newspapers and to television. But for every story about teen gambling that makes it into the newspapers, there are thousands more that go unreported. While some teens gamble safely, easily, and without any apparent problems, others find their gambling leads to unexpected problems. Here are the stories of some real-life teens who got in trouble from their gambling:

- A Washington State teen girl was arrested after stealing a mint coin collection from the family for whom she babysat. She said she stole the coins to get money to gamble on video games. (*USA Today*, "Is Your Teen Addicted to Gambling?" by J. Taylor Buckley, April 5, 1995, pages 4–5D.)

- A Massachusetts high school student "broke into" his own house four times to steal television sets and silverware. He smashed windows to make it look like a thief had entered. He sold the valuables to cover gambling losses. (*USA Today*, "Is Your Teen Addicted to Gambling?" by J. Taylor Buckley, April 5, 1995, pages 4–5D.)

- A New England teen got a $6,000 bonus to join a professional sports team, but he gambled it away at the racetrack. He then stole from his family to pay for his habit. (*USA Today*, "Is Your Teen Addicted to Gambling?" by J. Taylor Buckley, April 5, 1995, pages 4–5D.)

- A 17-year-old New York teen skipped school, lost $11,000 at Atlantic City blackjack tables, and returned home to try to kill himself by overdosing on pills. Fortunately, he survived. (*USA Today*, "Is Your Teen Addicted to Gambling?" by J. Taylor Buckley, April 5, 1995, pages 4–5D.)

- An 18-year-old student was charged with running a $1,500-a-week sports betting ring from the hallways and classrooms of Shawnee High School in Medford, New Jersey. A student called the police and turned his classmate in because another student had made a joke bet of $7,000, and the teen bookie was holding him to it. (*The Trentonian*, "Student's Huge Bet Would Have Had Big Payoff," by Judy DeHaven, Trenton, New Jersey, December 14, 1993, page 3.)

- A 16-year-old boy won some money at a bowling tournament, took his stake to the Atlantic City casinos, and somehow got in to gamble. At first, he managed to parlay the money into several thousand dollars—but then he lost it all. Apparently as a result of this experience, he got hooked on gambling; he opened credit accounts under family members' names and used cash advances from the credit cards to gamble. In a year, he amassed a debt of $20,000. At 20, he was serving time in a Pennsylvania federal prison for credit-card fraud. ("The Diceman Cometh: Will Gambling Be a Bad Bet for Your Town?" by Ronald A. Reno, in *Policy Review: The Journal of American Citizenship,* March–April 1996, pages 1–7.)

- In Colombo, Sri Lanka (an island nation formerly known as Ceylon, located south of India), more than 100 slot machines were seized due to underage gambling. The police sent a special team to mount the raids on the jackpot centers because numerous complaints had been made that schoolchildren were seen in illegal gambling establishments during school hours. (XINHUA news agency, via Individual Inc., a web news database, April 2, 1997.)

- A mother brought her 12-year-old daughter to a casino in Maryland Heights, Missouri. The mother knew that children under 18 were not allowed in casinos, so she gave her daughter fake identification. When the girl tried to place a bet, her mother was located and arrested. The casino was fined $250,000 for not properly checking the girl's ID at the door. Three employees were fired for approving the girl's ID. The mother was released with no charges filed, although she could have also been charged with endangerment of a child. (From "Casino Is Fined Over Bet By Child," by Fred Faust, *St. Louis Missouri, Post-Dispatch,* March 12, 1997, page 4.)

- A 16-year-old boy was just about to jump off the roof of his apartment building when his mother discovered him. He said he wanted to kill himself because he owed $800 to a bookmaker and payment was overdue. Since he was an excellent athlete and student, no one suspected that he had gambling problems. ("Helping Teen-age Compulsive Gamblers," by Annette Wexler, *The New York Times,* December 11, 1994, page 26.)

Sam's brother has read about problems with teen gambling, and he wants to help his brother. He suggested to him that if he wants more money, instead of gambling, he should get a job or do chores for neighbors. Sam discussed the possibilities with the people living on his street. Together, they made a list of the chores he could do and the amount of money neighbors might pay him to do them. The chart listed pulling weeds, washing windows, cleaning garages, painting bathrooms, and many others. After a few months, Sam had made $50 from doing chores. Sam was happy to have found a way to earn pocket money, without having to gamble.

Andrea feels bad about Tom's attempted suicide. She wonders if there was anything she could have said or done to prevent him from taking so many pills. She tries to think if Tom might have given her any indication that he was seriously upset over his gambling problems, but she can't think of any. Andrea decides that, in the future, she will tell the school guidance counselor if she hears Tom saying things that cause concern.

Mike realizes he could have been the one who was beat up at the Super Bowl party. He knows he often quarrels with the guys about bets. This incident is a "wake-up call" for Mike. He decides he has to cut back on his gambling and that he must come up with a plan to pay off his bookie.

Sports Gambling

Sports fans everywhere love to root for their favorite teams, whether in person or as part of a television audience. And many of those fans like to gamble on the outcome of the games. In most places, sports betting between friends is legal. Only in Las Vegas is it legally permissible to bet on sports in public. Gambling on sports events is strictly limited; however, most sports gambling activities are illegal. Sports professionals are not allowed to bet on any games, or they risk suspension or a lifetime ban. For nonprofessionals, the illegality starts when a third party—a bookmaker, or bookie—gets a piece of the action. Then, betting on sports becomes a crime.

Many sports superstars have had problems regarding gambling. In the past few years, Michael Jordan and Pete Rose are among the sports figures who have had allegations of illegal gambling or compulsive gambling made against them. Even as far back as 1919, eight members of the Chicago White Sox baseball team, including the national star Shoeless Joe Jackson, were banned for their lifetime from the game for illegal gambling.

Illegal sports betting is a huge underground business that is on the rise in America. Sports enthusiasts wager billions of dollars with illegal bookmakers. Experts think that illegal sports betting has grown so much because so many games are carried on television, especially now that there are hundreds of satellite cable stations. Some experts even think that so many people *want* to view sports to such an extent *because* they are betting on the games. The growing acceptance of legal gambling is also a reason illegal sports gambling has grown. Even though betting with bookies on sports is illegal, police have not spent a lot of time and money enforcing laws against gambling.

While the increase in sports betting makes game-fixing a possibility, the likelihood of that happening has gone down. Game-fixing is when team members are given bribes by gamblers to influence the outcome of a game. Today, professional athletes earn such high salaries that they have little reason to take bribes.

In 1997 the National Council on Compulsive Gambling estimated that illegal sports betting amounted to $84 billion in 1995 and that it might top $100 billion by the end of 1997. By contrast, *US News and World Report* says that America's illegal drug trade is much less, at around $49 billion per year.

There are many stories in the news about teens and professional athletes getting involved in sports gambling. Here are some of them:

- Student bookies at the University of Alabama described their operation on HBO in November 1996. Of 40 campuses that HBO queried, all had active student gambling operations. HBO used undercover cameras to shoot the Alabama bookies as they took bets and made collection calls. HBO estimates that the bookies on the Alabama campus gross $500,000 a year. One bookie said he actually takes in as much as $14,000 a week, mostly from students making bets of $20 to $25.
- On March 1, 1995, Nutley, New Jersey police busted a student-run sports gambling operation at Nutley High School. The ring took bets as high as $1,000 and used threats of violence and kidnapping to get losers to pay. They even kidnapped a 14-year-old student who was not able to pay, drove him to a dangerous neighborhood in Newark, and dropped him off. After executing search warrants at the homes of the three youths, police confiscated records listing bets with students as well as a list of the bettors and their phone numbers, along with the home numbers of organized crime bookmaking offices in New York City. ("Gambling Fever Infecting New Jersey Teens," by P. L. Wycoff and Patrick Jenkins, *The Newark Star-Ledger,* March 5, 1995, no page number available.)
- On November 7, 1996, Boston College suspended 13 football players for betting. Three of them were suspended for the entire school year, losing their scholarships and facing a permanent ban from ever playing college or professional football. Three other players were permanently barred from the football team but allowed to stay in school. In addition, in January 1997, eight Boston College seniors were permanently suspended for illegal betting, and disciplinary action began against at least 20 others. The student bookies all admitted to taking

bets, totalling close to $5,000 a week. As a result, student dormitory advisers were required to undergo a workshop on the dangers of gambling. Like most colleges Boston College had not previously had any rules on gambling in its student handbook, but after this incident, it moved to add them. ("Boston College Students Suspended for Gambling," Associated Press, January 15, 1997.)

- In the 1980s, former Colts quarterback Art Schlichter was suspended from the NFL when he sought help from league officials for his compulsive gambling. He owed $150,000 in gambling debts and was scheduled to go for treatment for his gambling addiction at the Baltimore Compulsive Gambling Center. However, in March 1997, he was arrested for violating conditions of his probation because he was involved in bank fraud. He faces many years in prison. (Associated Press, March 19, 1997.)

- In March 1997, law enforcement officials broke up a major organized-crime-run sports betting operation in New York City. The police said they had deliberately timed the raids for when betting was heavy, with the National Collegiate Athletic Association (NCAA) basketball tournament under way. Members of the betting ring were part of the Gambino crime family. The police announced that the public should not bet with Mafia-run gambling operations because their profits often go to finance mob activities like trafficking in guns and drugs. ("25 Arrested in Crackdown on Mob-Run Betting Ring," by Joseph Fried, *New York Times*, March 19, 1997).

- Oregon has a state-sponsored Sports Action game—a kind of lottery—that allows wagering on professional football. The NCAA basketball committee refused to consider the Portland Rose Garden arena for tournament games because of this. They did not want to hold tournaments in places where it is legal to wager on sports events because it sent a bad message. The NCAA objects to sports betting because it is illegal everywhere in the country except Las Vegas.

- Albert Belle, a Chicago White Sox player with a five-year, $55 million contract, said under oath that he lost as much as $40,000 gambling on sports. Belle said gambling is common among athletes and that money often changes hands in the locker room. (Associated Press, March 30, 1997.)

Gambling and Politics

Federal and state politicians are very interested in gambling and its effects on our way of life. Most elected officials have an opinion on gambling, which they often voice as part of their campaign. Very often, a politician's position on gambling has a lot to do with whether gambling is legal in his or her state. Laws regulating gambling are decided by each state; there are very few federal laws on the matter. Different communities have different opinions of gambling. Politicians from various states often argue with each other about whether gambling is good or bad for a community.

A New Law to Study Gambling
To resolve some of these arguments, the federal government decided in 1997 that we need to know more about gambling's effect on society. The U.S. House of Representatives passed a bill establishing a two-year commission to study the effects of gambling, including political contributions, advertising, crime, and Internet betting. Its mandate is to produce a "comprehensive legal and factual study of the social and economic impacts of gambling" on governments, communities, families, and social institutions. The panel has the power to hold hearings and subpoena documents. The commission will also look into:

- existing federal, state, local, and Native American policies and practices with regard to gambling
- the relationship between crime and gambling

- pathological or problem gambling and its impact on society
- the impact of gambling and advertising on families, business, and society
- gambling by electronic means, including gambling on the Internet

However, there is no requirement for individual states to adopt or even consider any of the findings of the study. States will retain their power to regulate gambling.

Gambling on the Internet

One of the issues that the commission will study is gambling on the Internet. Many Internet gambling sites are already offering bingo, lotteries, virtual casinos, and other types of betting. Most of the sites require using real money to play, although some are just for fun. Some sites do let people play for free for a while, hoping to get them hooked. The government and politicians are most interested in examining the sites that require payment in the form of checks, money orders, or credit cards. Most teens do not have their own lines of credit, and authorities are concerned that teens will take their parents' credit cards and run up large gambling debts.

Many companies have invested a lot of money in putting gambling sites on the Internet, yet lawmakers are not sure whether Internet gambling is legal. The government is taking a close look at the federal Interstate Wire Act of 1961, which they believe might be invoked to prohibit Internet gambling. This act was created to discourage illegal bookmaking. It forbids anyone in the gaming industry from using interstate or international phone lines to transmit information assisting the placement of bets. In addition, gambling over phone lines is illegal in most states. Since the Internet is transmitted over phone lines in most places, many politicians think these laws might apply. Knowing of this law, many online betting sites have avoided confronting it by running the Internet sites from outside the United States.

The federal government contends, on the other hand, that the fact of an Internet gambling site being run from a foreign country does not make it legal for a U.S. citizen to gamble on it. The U.S. government holds that gambling must be legal at both ends of the phone line in order for it to be legal in this country.

Legal or not, online gambling is risky business. While standard casinos are regulated to make sure they are trustworthy, most online gambling sites are not. For this reason, experts predict that Internet gambling will probably lean toward betting on events whose outcomes are widely publicized, in order to prevent cheating. For example, it is simple to check the outcome of presidential elections or horse races. By contrast, it would be hard, if not impossible, to know if "cyber dice" or "cyber slot machines" are rigged.

In May 1997, the state of Missouri ordered a company that offers Internet gambling to stop taking bets from Missouri residents and to pay thousands of dollars in penalties. The state government said the company violated state gambling and consumer laws. Many more of these kinds of lawsuits will probably take place before the issue of Internet gambling is decided.

Is Gambling Good or Bad for Society?

Another issue the commission will study is the effects of gambling on society. Should the government host lotteries when people may become addicted to them? Since the government makes a lot of money from taxing the profits of gambling organizations, should we be concerned that the government is relying too heavily on this money? Should we worry that the government, which is supposed to represent the people, may be too much in favor of gambling?

When gambling laws come up for review by the government, there is a lot of lobbying for and against them. The

American Gaming Association and casinos always lobby in favor of gambling. These organizations and businesses try to influence elected officials to vote for gambling. However, those opposed to gambling or who are not sure if gambling is good for society, don't have a national organization to represent their views nor to spend to try to influence legislators.

There are complex economic issues to consider as well. Gambling companies claim that gambling is good for the economy, but compulsive gambling experts insist that gambling is bad for the economy. Supporters of gambling say it creates jobs in casinos, nearby restaurants, and other businesses—all of which are good for the economy. They say the government can use the money it makes from gambling to spend on things like education, building new roads, and maintaining parks and playgrounds. For example, Tunica County, Mississippi, which had been the poorest county in the United States, became a booming business center after 25 casinos were built there. The area is now compared to Las Vegas and Atlantic City, two other areas that benefited from casinos. Since the 1980s, some Native American tribes have benefited from gambling as well, by having casinos on reservations. In addition, gambling proponents say there are many other things that have the potential to affect people negatively, such as alcohol, tobacco, and even fatty fast food, and these things are still legal.

Anti-gambling people say that gambling is bad for the economy. They say that the money the government makes from gambling is not being spent on improving the quality of life, and that no one is actually keeping track of exactly how tax money raised from gambling is being spent. They say that lottery dollars spent by poor people leave their neighborhood and that they rarely see any benefits from the government paid for by gambling revenues. They say that gambling increases crime, which is not good for society. They say that the huge number of people who get addicted to gambling costs government more money in treating the addictions than the government receives in lottery revenues. Finally, people who are against gambling say that government should not finance itself with the money of people who buy lottery tickets. They argue that government should not willfully encourage people to gamble when the money they spend to do so should be allocated to food, shelter, and clothing.

Gambling and Political Contributions

Often, the gambling industry contributes money to elected officials' campaigns with the expectation that, when elected, the officials will help to pass laws that favor the gambling industry. The commission will study how much money is being given to legislators by gambling businesses. Many elected officials think that there should be a law that prohibits politicians from accepting money from businesses related to gambling—businesses that donate millions of dollars each year to political parties. A report in the August 1997 issue of *Mother Jones,* a magazine known for its investigative reporting, revealed that gambling lobbyists have given at least $100 million to state politicians over the last five years and at least $6.4 million to federal politicians in the last four years.

However, politicians also accept money from alcohol and tobacco companies, to which many people also object. Yet the idea that any group should be denied access to government officials is problematic in our society. Thus, it is not likely that these laws will be passed any time soon.

In the past few years, referendums on election ballots in many areas have asked people to decide if they want to allow casinos or other types of gambling in their state. Most of these referendums failed to pass. People are starting to vote against legalized gambling because they see the problems it can bring.

Gambling and Advertising

The commission will study the effects of gambling advertising on our society. It will consider whether the gambling industry should be allowed to advertise at all, to what degree, or in what ways. It will examine who should fund compulsive gambling programs. It will decide if gambling businesses should take more action to prevent compulsive gambling. Gambling advertising will be explored in detail in the next chapter.

3

Making Decisions About Gambling

Dave's decision to opt out of his friend's poker game led to a lot of big changes he didn't expect. Even though he went to the games—he just didn't play—after a while, the guys didn't want him hanging around watching. They were afraid he was looking at their cards and sending signals—in other words, cheating. The guys didn't actually accuse him of cheating, but Dave knew that's what they were thinking.

Dave really liked being around his friends, but since he sensed they didn't feel the same way about him, he stopped going to the games. At first, he felt sad and lonely that his friends were having fun without him. But he realized that he enjoyed not having the pressure of gambling. He made a special effort to make other plans with the same group of friends. They played basketball together a lot, and in the summer they went to the town pool together.

Sam has decided he has been so lucky with his Oscar and election pool, that he should make better use of his "luck" skills. At a bookstore, he sees a book entitled *How to Dream Your Lucky Numbers,* and on impulse, he buys it. The book tells him how he can use his dreams to predict winning lottery numbers. Sam tries the technique. He has a dream that his lucky numbers are flying overhead in the sky, attached to an airplane. As soon as he wakes up, he writes the numbers down on a pad he's kept next to his bed just for this purpose. Then, Sam checks the winning lottery numbers for the next day. The numbers are completely different from the ones he dreamed. Sam is glad he didn't actually waste his money on a lottery ticket. He is mad at himself, however, for spending $10 on the dumb book.

When Andrea goes to visit her nine-year-old cousin Brandon, he begs Andrea to walk with him to the corner store to buy him some candy. Andrea agrees this would be fun, and they go to the store. But when they arrive, Brandon is not interested in the bubble gum Andrea wants to buy him. Brandon wants Andrea to buy him a pack of baseball cards. Brandon is attracted to the fancy, limited edition "chase cards" that might be hidden inside the pack. These are cards that are either fancy, for example, with holograms or stickers, or that show a famous player whose card is in very short supply. Andrea gives in and buys Brandon the pack of baseball cards. Excitedly, Brandon tears it open, only to be disappointed that there is no chase card inside.

Mike is not having much success in cutting down on his gambling—one minute he considers quitting, and the next minute he abandons the idea. He wishes he had someone to talk to about his problem, like his father. But he can't talk about his problem to his father, because he is never around. Mike knows his father sits in front of the slot machines at the nearby casino every night with a cup of quarters in one hand and a complimentary alcoholic drink in the other. All day in school, Mike thinks about how he can get more money to gamble. He doesn't want to break into another soda machine. That was too risky. Then he remembers that his mother keeps cash in her dresser "for a rainy day." He decides to take it to the casino. He is sure he can win enough to replace the money back even before his mother notices.

Our society gives confusing messages about teen gambling. One message is that it is illegal for teens to gamble. All states have laws that make gambling by anyone under the age of 18 illegal. This includes buying lottery tickets, betting at horse races, and betting at casinos.

However, there are many subtle ways that our society contradicts these laws. Open the newspaper and you'll see ads aimed at families for gambling meccas like Las Vegas and Atlantic City. Go to a fund-raiser in the community, and bingo or other gambling games will be featured. Winning lottery numbers announced on television broadcast to everyone that gambling is acceptable, exciting, and worthwhile. And many respected adults regularly bet on sports events with a bookie, which is illegal.

This chapter will help you decide for yourself how you feel about gambling. You will have to decide if risking money makes sense, or is frightening, or exciting. Your conclusions may be different than those of your family and friends.

Dave's decision to stop playing cards, for example, was a different decision than the one his friends had made. Although Dave still enjoys playing poker for money, he made up his mind to stop, because he wanted to spend his cash on different things—and in a different way than his friends. If Dave had lots of money, he would be able to play poker *and* buy the CDs and concert tickets that he wants. But like most people, Dave doesn't have enough money to buy everything he wants. In Dave's case, giving up gambling has been a purely practical decision—a choice to buy other kinds of entertainment with his money. In fact, Dave's friends don't have a lot of cash, either. And soon after Dave quit gambling, Steve decided to stop playing poker too. In their case, gambling wasn't a psychological problem. But Dave and Steve did come to feel it was an activity that was not beneficial to them.

Sam was experimenting with a new kind of gambling when he moved on from running betting pools to picking lottery numbers from his dreams. What he learned from this experience is how unlikely it is that he would ever choose the winning numbers. As Sam discovered, lots of books say they will help you win at gambling—at casinos and tracks, as well as at lotteries. Often, these books can make readers feel like it is easy to win and that it is their fault if they don't.

Brandon's attraction to chase cards in baseball packs may seem innocent. For most people, the cards are a harmless, pleasant way to pass the time. Purchasers may feel a sense of excitement when they open a new package—a little disappointment if they don't win, and a big thrill if they do. Basically, though, the cards are not a significant part of the lives of the people who buy them.

For some people, though, the chase cards can become a far bigger preoccupation. These people may find that their mood is affected for several hours, first by looking forward to buying the cards, then by dealing with depression and a nagging sense of loss when they don't win.

Andrea didn't think it was fun to spend her money on something that disappointed her cousin—but even more, these kinds of games are really gambling. The three elements that define gambling come into play with chase cards —cost, chance, and potential payoff. The payoff is that some chase cards, because they are limited edition and rare, may eventually be worth thousands of dollars. In fact, an article in *US News* on December 2, 1996 said that chase cards violate a gambling law called RICO, for Racketeer Influenced and Corrupt Organizations Act.

Baseball cards have been around for many years, and cards for certain players have always been more desirable and rare—to encourage customers to keep buying the gum that comes with the cards as well as their hope of getting the card they want. Many people don't see the difference between these long-accepted cards and chase cards. But chase cards are heavily advertised—some would say misleadingly. The advertising makes it seem like the chase cards are easy to get, whereas they are actually very rare. In response to this criticism, the baseball card industry has begun to print the odds of finding a chase card on each pack. However, for people who are concerned about compulsive gambling, this very practice proves that chase cards really are a kind of lottery—a gamble on buying the winning card. As Dr. Sheila Blume, an addiction expert, quoted in the article says, "These are called chase cards, and chasing losses is what compulsive gamblers do." Thus, in Dr. Blume's opinion, kids who use their entire allowance to buy the packs and then tear them open in a frenzy to see whether there is a chase card enclosed are actually exhibiting the behavior of compulsive gamblers.

Your Views About Money

Your attitudes about money play a large part in how you feel about gambling. In this section, you'll have a chance to explore how you feel about money—about earning, saving, and spending it. This can help you decide how your view of money fits in with your views on gambling. You may decide that gambling is just a waste of money. Or you may think that spending a little money on gambling is a fun way to pass the time, like going to a movie or a concert.

Other people prefer to buy things they can use for a long time, like athletic shoes, jewelry, or a leather jacket. Some people believe in spending money on different types of experiences. These people may like to travel, eat in restaurants, and attend different types of workshops and events. When their money is spent, they may not have anything physical to show for it, but they have a lot of fascinating memories.

Many teens start to gamble because they see it as a way to get more money when they don't have enough. Some teens think that by gambling they'll strike it rich and be able to buy whatever they want, perhaps even help their families get out of debt or make a special purchase. Too often, though, people who make little money, like teens, fall into the trap of spending a higher proportion of their income on gambling than higher income earners.

Everyone Wants Money

Have you ever heard one friend say to another, "I have too much money. I don't need all this money?" Does that sound far-fetched? It certainly does. Most of us feel like we never have enough money. Everyone not only wants money—in today's society, everyone *needs* money. Money is what we use in exchange for goods and services we can't produce on our own. There are many things that money can't buy, such as love, respect, kindness, and friendship. But many things we need in order to live must be bought with money.

We need food, so unless we grow our own food, we need money to buy food from the people who do make, grow, or sell it. We need a place to live, and unless we build it ourselves, we—or our families—need to pay rent, or a mortgage and taxes. We need clothing, and unless we weave fabric and sew it ourselves, we need to buy clothes from a store.

There are always a few things we want or need that we don't have. In fact, one of the problems with money is making the distinctions between what we need versus what we want. We all need food, but some types of food cost more money than others. Do we need the more expensive food, or do we just want it? Many teens like to wear athletic shoes, but some designer brands cost more than others. If an unknown brand is comfortable, why do so many people choose to buy the more expensive brands?

Most of the time, advertising and peer pressure influence people to buy things they want, rather than what they need. It is this feeling of wanting more money that often leads people to gambling to get more of it.

Ways to Get Money

As appealing as money is, it is not easy to get. There are only five ways to get money, and not all of them are legal or likely. (We don't include borrowing money on this list, because you still need to get money to pay it back, often with interest. Interest is money that is charged for the privilege of borrowing it. For example, if a person borrows $1,000 from a bank, the bank will charge interest, of perhaps $150. The person will then have to pay the bank back the $1,000 plus $150, for a total of $1,150.) Here are the five ways to get money. Which ways do you use to get money?

1. **Earn It:** This is the most common way to obtain money. Earning money by performing a service, or by creating and selling a product, is socially and ethically acceptable, as long as the job or product is legal. Work provides feelings of satisfaction and gives you self-esteem.

   You can earn money by getting a job, if you are old enough to work in your state. You can earn money even if you are not old enough to get certain jobs, by doing chores, baby-sitting, selling crafts at fairs, and many other ways. Look for books in your library or bookstore for ideas on ways that teens can earn money.

Earning money by working does have its responsibilities and possible problems. If you work, you need to make sure you still have enough time to do your homework, after-school activities, and to do chores at home. You may have less time to spend with friends, family, and just being by yourself.

2. **Inherit It:** Some teens inherit money when a relative dies. Most teens do not obtain money this way.

3. **Get Money as a Gift:** Teens often are given cash as gifts for birthdays and special occasions. While this way of obtaining money is usually welcome, it is rather unpredictable and infrequent.

4. **Steal It:** Stealing is against the law and is ethically wrong. Teens who steal may do it because it is exciting and may result in more money than working at a job. But stealing has the potential to hurt many people in many ways. Most people don't want to live in a world where people steal from one another. Getting caught can land a person in jail, and in violent situations, can lead to serious injury and death.

5. **Win It:** This is where gambling comes in. However, you must have money in order to win money at gambling. If you win money, it can be exciting and fun. Losing, however, is disappointing and frustrating.

Another way to win money is by winning a sweepstakes or contest in which you do not have to risk money, only a stamp or a phone call. The odds of winning a sweepstakes are very small. Also, teens are not legally eligible for most sweepstakes.

Ways to Use Money

Once you get money, there are only a few things you can do with it. Which of the following do you like to do with your money?

1. **Save or Invest It:** Do you like to put money in the bank? If you don't have a bank account, why not open one soon? The bank will pay you interest on the money. Many banks have special savings accounts for children and teens, for which you don't need a lot of money to open the account or have a minimum balance. Even if you open an account like this with only $10 and put in $5 a month, you will be amazed at how quickly your money will grow. Some teens, together with their parents, put money in investments such as money-market funds, stocks, college savings accounts, and other types of accounts to save for the future.

2. **Spend It:** Some teens need to spend their money on basics like food because their parents don't earn enough to supply food for the family. Other teens spend their money on things they want because their parents earn enough to provide the things they need.

    Things that teens like to spend their money on include movie tickets, renting videos and games, video and computer games, music tapes and CDs, jeans and T-shirts, snack food, sports equipment, magazines and books, and much more. How do you like to spend your money?

3. **Donate It to Charity:** Many teens like to give some of their money to charities that provide services for people in need.

4. **Gamble It:** This way of using money is illegal for teens, although many types of gambling are legal for adults. The rest of this chapter will help you decide whether gambling is worth the risk.

How to Analyze Lottery Advertising

Are you aware of the amount of this week's lottery jackpot? If you are, it is because of the millions of dollars your state government spent to advertise the jackpot. State lotteries are among the largest and most aggressive advertisers in the country, according to a July 14, 1996 *New York Times* article entitled "Muting the Lotteries' Perfect Pitch." Federal law prevents casinos from advertising their gambling games; they are only allowed to advertise their food and entertainment. This is because federal laws apply to casinos but not to lotteries.

State lotteries spend millions on advertising to encourage people to think they can win huge jackpots. Some lottery ads even send the message that actually working for money is a waste of time compared with gambling. Many people say that lottery ads contribute to compulsive gambling. Both compulsive casino gamblers and those who gamble through the lottery have a great fear that their "lucky number" will fall on a day they didn't bet. Lottery ads play to this fear. For example, many ads say "don't forget to play every day." Other ads show people who lost because their number came up on a day they didn't play.

In some cases, lottery advertising can be deceptive. That's because lottery ads are the only form of advertising to which state and federal truth-in-advertising standards do not apply. The standards require that ads be truthful, and the government checks on the ads to make sure they are. Lottery ads are not required to state the odds against winning. Lottery advertising only shows the big winners, never the millions of losers. Ads for other contests and sweepstakes are required to clearly state the odds against winning. The odds for the lottery *can* be obtained if you ask the seller of the tickets, but they don't have to be mentioned in television ads, radio ads, and on billboards.

Compulsive gambling experts say that lottery ads lure low-income families to spend a great deal of money on lottery tickets. However, lottery industry people dispute this. It has also been found that some food stamp recipients sell their stamps to buy lottery tickets.

Other lottery advertising techniques that have been criticized include indicating what imaginary winners might do with their winnings; using inaccurate language regarding winning, implying that if you buy a ticket you certainly will be a winner; and praising people who buy lottery tickets while putting down those who don't.

Some states have passed laws forbidding these types of ads, and some states are beginning to change their lottery ads. They are creating ads that avoid raising unrealistic expectations and stress that the lottery's main purpose is to raise money for education. The Virginia state lottery officials created a very different type of advertising: a "Play Responsibly" public relations campaign, warning people of the risks of compulsive gambling. But most state ad agencies defend the ads, saying they give people permission to believe they can win and that lotteries raise money for the community. They run ads that say, for example, "When Colorado plays, everybody wins," and "The Missouri Lottery: it makes life a little richer for all of us."

States say that lottery money goes to pay for schools and parks, but critics say that most of the money doesn't go where politicians say it is going. Lottery money usually goes to a general fund, similar to the way taxes are handled. However, many people think that taxes are more honestly raised. In addition, communities can decide how tax money will be spent, but not how lottery money will be spent.

Here are some things that lottery ads say. Can you tell why some people might consider them deceptive? Do you think they are deceptive?

- All you need is dollar and a dream
- Hey, you never know
- We won't stop until everyone's a millionaire
- Sooner or later you're gonna win
- Somebody's always winning
- Play Lotto. The odds be with you

To counter gambling advertising, some Minnesota organizations that help compulsive gamblers are creating their own ads. These ads and posters bring attention to the downside of gambling, especially for teens. Here are some examples:

"You don't have to do drugs to get hooked by a dealer," is a poster with a picture of a stressed person holding five cards, playing poker. This poster is by the Minnesota Compulsive Gambling Hotline.

"Thousands of Minnesota teenagers are addicted to this kind of pot." This poster by the Minnesota Compulsive Gambling Hotline shows people sitting at a table and gambling. The "pot" is not marijuana, but a gambling "pot": a pile of money sitting in the middle of a card table.

"It's 10 P.M. Do you know where your parents are?" A poster of the Minnesota Compulsive Gambling Hotline has these words over a photo of a casino.

"Just because you're sixteen doesn't mean you can't be up to your eyeballs in debt." This poster by the Minnesota Department of Health Services, Mental Health Division, shows a picture of a jack of diamonds, just with the head above the eyeballs showing.

"Where to gamble your last quarter." The Gambling Problems Resource Center in Minnesota has a poster with these words over a picture of a public telephone and gambling hot line number.

"Problem drinkers are often in a position to become problem gamblers," a poster by the Minnesota Compulsive Gambling Hotline shows two pictures. The first is of a man sitting in a bar. The second shows the same man sitting in the same bar, now with a slot machine. This ad is meant to show that in places where slot machines are allowed in bars, people who are addicted to alcohol may also become addicted to gambling.

The Odds of Winning

Dave, Sam, Andrea, and Mike all have opinions about the odds of winning with gambling. When Dave was playing cards, he nearly always lost. He did not have a good "poker face" and found it hard to disguise his thoughts about the cards he was dealt. So Dave came to feel that the odds were always against him. That's why he stopped playing.

Sam believes that if you stack the odds in your favor, it is fun and profitable to gamble. When he devises his Oscar pools, he makes sure he knows a lot about the contenders. This way, his guesses are educated, not just wild chances. He understands that there is still a large element of risk.

Andrea feels that no amount of risk is worth it when it comes to her money. No matter what the odds, she would rather use her money in ways she knows will bring her pleasure, never disappointment. She would always rather take five dollars and buy new makeup, pizza, magazines, or perhaps rent a movie rather than buy a lottery ticket or a hand in a card game.

Mike knows the odds are stacked against him when he gambles, but he doesn't care. He always believes that the next game will be the lucky one that will win him back all his money. Knowing that the odds are stacked against you but not caring, even when spending a lot of money on bets, is one sign a person is a compulsive gambler.

People like Mike who gamble a lot sometimes think that dice, quarters, or roulette wheels have a memory. They unrealistically think that if they flipped a quarter three times and it came up heads, that next time it will be tails. But the chances of getting tails on the fourth toss is 50 percent, the same as the chances of getting either heads or tails on any toss. The quarter doesn't "remember" how it landed the other times. Each toss is completely independent of any other toss.

Chance Versus Skill

Face it—there is no way that casinos or lotteries can give people good odds, or they would not be able to stay in business. Lotteries are based on chance only, as are casino games like roulette and bingo. Other games, like poker and blackjack, add an element of skill, so the odds go up slightly in the player's favor.

In games of pure chance, you can guess what the outcome will be, but you cannot influence the outcome with skill or will. Games of chance operate on the law of averages. If you take a quarter and flip it 20 times, the law of averages says that approximately half of the tosses will be heads and half tails. Try it yourself and see what happens.

The law of averages does not always work the way you think it will. Try to think of it more as an average than a law. The more times you toss the coin, the closer you will come to approximating the 50/50 average, but there is no guarantee that the results will be perfect. Try this experiment. Flip a coin 20 times, making a pretend $2 bet on each toss. If you called heads or tails correctly, you win $2. If not, you lose $2. Did you win money, lose money, or come out even in the end?

Other games of chance, like roulette, also operate on the law of averages, but since there are more options (as opposed to only two options on a coin), the odds are much lower that a particular number will come up. If a roulette wheels has 40 slots, the law of averages says that the ball will fall into a particular slot, say number 10, only one time in 40 spins of the wheel.

Dice rely on chance too. Each die has six sides, so chances are one in six that you will throw a certain number. If you throw three dice, the chances are 216 to 1 against you that you will turn up a specific number. The odds of winning lottery numbers games are worse—six number games give you only a 1 in 10 million chance; seven numbers, 1 in 100 million.

In casinos, the payoff of any particular game is much more complicated than the tossing of a coin, so we will not go into the math here. Mathematicians do say that you can win money gambling in a casino, but only in the short run. The longer you play, the larger the chances are that you will lose.

Some players think that the Random Number Generator, the computer that now controls slot machines, has an actual personality. They think that if they put their quarter in at a certain time, or in a certain way, or if they pull the handle a certain way, or if they follow some other superstition, it will help them win a jackpot. But the Random Number Generator cannot be influenced by any of these things.

Many times, when people buy a lottery ticket or play a keno game, they do not understand how dismal their chances of winning are at these games of chance. Other times, people understand, but decide that the money they paid is a fair price for being entertained and being given a chance to win, however small. But many people who have won money at a casino find it very hard to stop playing and go home with their cash. They want to keep playing in an attempt to win more and often end up losing what they won. It takes an enormous amount of discipline to quit while you're ahead, even for people who are not addicted to gambling.

Gambling Laws in Your State

Some states, like New Jersey, allow casinos and horse racing and have state lotteries. Other states, like Utah, don't allow any type of gambling, even church bingo. The position of most states on gambling lies somewhere in between. Your exposure to various types of gambling will be different depending on what state you live in.

The United States does not have federal laws defining what types of gambling are legal in the country as a whole, although no states allow gambling with a bookie. Here is a list of the types gambling that are legal in each state in the United States. The list was taken from a book titled *The Absolute Beginner's Guide to Gambling.*

Charitable games are those that religious and other nonprofit organizations hold to raise money, as opposed to those that take place in for-profit casinos or state-sponsored lotteries. When the chart says "bingo on Indian reservations" that means bingo is the only gambling allowed. When the chart says "Indian reservation gaming," that means games in addition to bingo are allowed; this often means casinos on reservations are allowed. "Riverboats" means boats on which gambling games are played. Cardrooms are places where people can go to gamble on card games legally; they are like small casinos, but with only card games being played.

Legal Types of Gambling

Alabama: charitable games, horse/dog racing, bingo on Indian reservations

Alaska: charitable games

Arizona: charitable games, horse/dog racing, lottery, Indian reservation gaming

Arkansas: horse/dog racing

California: cardrooms, charitable games, horse racing, lottery, Indian reservation gaming

Colorado: cardrooms, casinos, charitable games, horse/dog racing, lottery, Indian reservation gaming

Connecticut: charitable games, horse/dog racing, lottery, Indian reservation gaming

Delaware: charitable games, horse racing, lottery

Florida: charitable games, horse/dog racing, bingo on Indian reservations

Georgia: charitable games, lottery

Hawaii: no gambling permitted

Idaho: horse/dog racing, lottery, bingo on Indian reservations

Illinois: charitable games, riverboats, horse/dog racing, lottery

Indiana: charitable games, horse racing, lottery

Iowa: cardrooms, charitable games, riverboats, horse/dog racing, lottery, Indian reservation gaming

Kansas: charitable games, horse/dog racing, lottery, bingo on Indian reservations

Kentucky: horse racing, lottery

Louisiana: cardrooms, casinos, charitable games, riverboats, horse/dog racing, lottery, Indian reservation gaming

Maine: charitable games, horse racing, lottery, bingo on Indian reservations

Maryland: charitable games, horse/dog racing, lottery

Massachusetts: charitable games, horse/dog racing, lottery

Michigan: charitable games, horse racing, lottery, Indian reservation gaming

Minnesota: charitable games, horse racing, lottery, Indian reservation gaming

Mississippi: charitable games, riverboats, horse/dog racing, Indian reservation gaming

Missouri: charitable games, riverboats, lottery; horse/dog racing allowed, but none are currently operating

Montana: cardrooms, charitable games, horse/dog racing, lottery, Indian reservation gaming

Nebraska: charitable games, horse/dog racing, lottery, bingo on Indian reservations

Nevada: cardrooms, casinos, charitable games, Indian reservation gaming, sports betting

New Hampshire: charitable games, horse/dog racing, lottery

New Jersey: casinos, charitable games, horse/dog racing, lottery

New Mexico: charitable games, horse/dog racing, bingo on Indian reservations

New York: charitable games, horse/dog racing, lottery, Indian reservation gaming

North Carolina: charitable games only

North Dakota: cardrooms, charitable games, horse/dog racing, Indian reservations permit mini-casinos with blackjack and pull tabs (scratch-off tickets)

Ohio: charitable games, horse/dog racing, lottery

Oklahoma: charitable games, horse/dog racing, bingo on Indian reservations

Oregon: cardrooms, charitable games, horse/dog racing, lottery, Indian reservation gaming

Pennsylvania: charitable games, horse/dog racing, lottery

Rhode Island: charitable games, horse/dog racing, lottery

South Carolina: charitable games only

South Dakota: cardrooms, casinos, charitable games, horse/dog racing, lottery, Indian reservation gaming

Tennessee: horse/dog racing only

Texas: charitable games, horse/dog racing, lottery, Indian reservation gaming

Utah: no gambling permitted

Vermont: charitable games, horse/dog racing, lottery

Virginia: charitable games, horse/dog racing, lottery

Washington: cardrooms, charitable games, horse/dog racing, lottery, Indian reservation gaming

Washington, D.C.:   charitable games, lottery

West Virginia: charitable games, horse/dog racing, lottery

Wisconsin: charitable games, horse/dog racing, lottery, Indian reservation gaming

Wyoming: charitable games, horse/dog racing, bingo on Indian reservations

American Indian–Run Gaming

Indian reservations are lands that have been retained by American Indian tribes from their ancestral lands or designated for their use by the U.S. government. Indian nations have a certain degree of sovereignty on these lands; state laws do not always apply. The state government's right to legislate and tax gaming on reservations is one area in question.

For numerous reasons, Indian reservations are among the poorest areas of the United States. With few resources or jobs, many tribal governments had to look for creative ways to boost their local economy. When state lotteries became common in the 1980s, many Indian tribes decided to sponsor bingo games—often with very high stakes—to raise money. At first, state governments challenged this, claiming it was illegal. But in 1988, Congress upheld legalized gambling on Indian reservations when it passed the Indian Gaming Regulatory Act. Some of the states in which there is now gambling on Indian reservations are Arizona, Florida, California, South Dakota, Wisconsin, Minnesota, Washington, New Mexico, and Connecticut.

Indian tribes use the money from gambling activities to fund tribal government programs, just like states use lottery money for government purposes. Gaming also helps the economy by providing thousands of jobs, encouraging tourism, and generating income for hotels and restaurants. For example, Foxwoods Casino run by the Mashantucket Pequot in Connecticut is now one of the state's biggest employers, creating jobs not just for Indians but for many local residents.

The National Indian Gaming Commission reported that in 1997, there were 115 tribes in 24 states running gambling businesses. This represents less than one third of all tribes and is only 5 percent of the total gambling industry in the United States. There are no statistics that tell how many Indian teens are gambling on reservations. The more gambling that there is, however, the more teens will be exposed to it, and the more chances are that some of them will develop gambling problems.

Underage Gambling Laws

As you can see, there is a wide variety of state laws regarding gambling. There are only two gambling issues that all states agree on, however. The first was already mentioned—that gambling with a bookmaker, or bookie, is illegal. This is because bookmakers historically have had ties to organized crime and because these underground activities are impossible for the government to oversee. The other issue that all states agree on is that gambling is illegal for minors. But who are minors? This definition also varies from state to state, and sometimes from game to game. The North American Think Tank on Youth Gambling Issues, which met in April 1995 at the Harvard Medical School Division on Addictions, summarized the laws on underage gambling: The minimum legal gambling ages vary from jurisdiction to jurisdiction, and from one gambling form to another within jurisdictions. For example, in most states, the minimum legal age for purchasing lottery tickets is 18, as is the minimum for pull tabs and pari-mutuel betting (racetrack betting). In some states, the minimum legal age for casino gambling is 18; in others, 21. In some states 18-year-olds may play the lottery or pulltabs legally, but may not gamble at casinos or place pari-mutuel bets. For example, in New Jersey, minimum age for placing bets at a racetrack is 18, but youths of 16 or 17 can legally gain admission to the track even if they are not accompanied by adults.

Sometimes even parents don't understand underage gambling laws. In an article titled "Vegas Keeps Its Chips on Adults," in October 21, 1996's *USA Today,* there is a quote from a security guard at a casino saying, "I've had adults ask me, where are the slot machines for the kids?"

If you would like to find out more about the gambling laws in your state, write or call your state attorney general's office or your state lottery and/or casino commission. These phone numbers can be found in the blue government section of your phone book. If your state has a site on the Internet, you may be able to find out phone numbers or information from the site. In this country, one has to comply with the laws even if one doesn't know what they are. So it's a good idea to find out what they are.

Behind the Laws

Why is it legal for adults to gamble but not teens? Legislators who wrote gambling laws that set the legal age took into account the fact that gambling responsibly requires a certain amount of self-control and judgment. While it is true that many teens are mature and have good self-control and judgment, many are still learning how to make tough decisions. It is also true that many adults display poor judgment and a lack of self-control, especially when it comes to gambling. But the government can't say it is all right for Andrea to gamble, because she is mature, but not for Mike, because he has a compulsive gambling problem. The government has decided to create the laws based on a cutoff age, much like laws about driving, drinking, and smoking.

Even though laws say minors can't gamble at legal gambling games, except in the case of casinos, governments rarely enforce these laws. It is likely that you know many teens who have bought lottery tickets, and none of them has ever been arrested for it. But just because teens aren't being arrested for breaking gambling laws, doesn't mean it is all right to ignore the laws. On the other hand, even if you are against gambling, you may think the age cutoffs in the laws are unfair.

Do you think there should there be tougher and more consistent enforcement of existing prohibitions against teen gambling? Or do you think teens should be allowed to gamble when and where they want to? Do you think there should be an age cutoff? At what age do you think that should be? Age 21? 18? 16? 12? 10? 5?

What do you think the government should do? One idea is for government to aggressively promote policies that prohibit payment of prizes to minors gambling illegally. This way, if a teen buys a lottery ticket that wins, the teen would not get the prize, because the ticket was bought illegally. Should there be tougher penalties against vendors who fail to enforce legal gambling age limits? Perhaps you can write a letter stating your ideas to your state legislators. They would be very interested in hearing your opinions.

Understand the Gambling Industry

To some people, gambling may mean playing poker with friends or making informal bets on football games. But beyond this, there are huge industries that make money from people who like to gamble—and from those who are addicted to it as well. It costs a lot of money to build, staff, and operate a casino. With this in mind, all gambling games are designed to favor the house, not the customers. The purpose of gambling is to provide money for the organization, whether it is a casino, the state, or a church. This is why gambling makes the casinos money, but not most of the players. The gaming industries, mainly the casino and the lottery industries, earn billions of dollars. To do this, they use marketing techniques that you should be aware of.

For starters, the gambling industry never uses the word "gambling." They call what they do "gaming." The industry knows that the word "gambling" can have negative connotations, so they avoid that word. They hope the word "gaming" will conjure up more wholesome images.

Casinos advertising aggressively. Then, once customers are inside a casino, there are many ways to keep them there. Free drinks and inexpensive food are offered. Slot machines are arranged in mazes so that people will get lost when they wander around. Casinos hope people will lose track of time trying to get out of these mazes and therefore spend more money. The stools at slot machines are designed to be so comfortable that people never want to stand up. Special lighting techniques create an atmosphere that is appealing.

Slot machines are programmed to make frequent small payoffs to entice people to keep chasing the dream of a large jackpot. However, in the long run, these small payoffs don't add up to as much as a customer is likely to spend. In fact, the jingling, jangling, clanging slot machines make more money for casinos than does any other form of gambling.

The men and women hired by the casino are often physically attractive, so that customers will feel drawn to them and enjoy being near them. Dealers are even trained never to cross their arms, as this body language subtly keeps people away.

There is a new trend to create tourist attractions out of casinos, to offer entertainment not just for adults but for children and the entire family. Many casinos now offer amusement rides, high-tech architecture and decorations, computer games, and lavish restaurants.

Should You Gamble or Not?

Knowing what you now do about gambling, you may be starting to develop an opinion about it. If you have never gambled, you may decide that you do not want to. Or, you may have decided that it might be fun to try when you are old enough. If you have gambled, you may decide to stop after losing money. Or, you may decide to continue as long as you don't spend too much money.

The reasons why people choose not to gamble are varied. Some people think it is foolish, or immoral, or a poor way to spend money. Others grew up in a family that never gambled, so it was not an activity in which they choose to engage. Still others choose not to gamble precisely because they grew up in a family that did have problems with gambling, and they want to avoid those problems themselves.

Some people who do choose to gamble do so because they consider it a fun way to spend time and money. They think the money they spend on gambling is worth the hours of entertainment they receive in return. Others who choose to gamble do so because they feel anxious, depressed, or overwhelmed at the idea of stopping.

But other than these personal experiences, is there any other place to look for guidance on whether or not to gamble? Often, people make decisions on whether or not to do things based on whether the government makes laws about it or whether their religion has moral guidance to offer. Some people may not choose to look to government or religion on the subject of gambling because both of them profit from it. Governments hold lotteries, and some religious institutions often hold charitable gambling games like bingo and raffles to raise funds. Others may feel their religion can aid their decisions. Whether you are Christian, Jewish, Muslim, Hindu, Buddhist, Shinto, or another religion, there are ideas in your religion that apply to gambling.

You can also clarify your own decisions independently about whether or not to gamble. Although laws and religion are good places to look for guidance, you need to examine how gambling affects you personally.

Think about both the positive and negative aspects of gambling. Gambling is exciting and provides a temporary escape from the boredom of everyday life. But if done to excess, it may get in the way of your relationships and school work.

You may come to the conclusion that gambling is fine as long as you are not hurting yourself or others. Or you may decide that the possibility of developing problems with gambling is a good reason to stay away from it.

Personal Gambling Guidelines

Suppose you have decided to gamble. If you do make the decision to gamble, you need to have some personal guidelines to call upon when needed. Take a look at these guidelines, which have been adapted from the work of Dr. Roger Svendsen, a compulsive gambling expert who has worked with teens, and think about whether you agree with them.

Gambling should be a personal choice. No one should feel pressured to gamble. If someone is pressuring you to gamble, that is the wrong reason to decide to gamble. A person should only gamble if he or she truly wants to, not because someone else is trying to convince him or her it is a good idea. If people decide to gamble, they should only gamble at games they like to play, and for which they understand the rules. They should observe others first, to make sure they know what is going on.

Decide how much you are willing to lose. If you decide to gamble, expect to spend on gambling about what you would spend on other entertainment, not more. Also, expect that you will lose more often than you will win. If you need your money for something else, don't use it to gamble. If the only money you have needs to be used for basics like food, clothing, shelter, education, or child care, then do not spend it on gambling. Set a limit before you leave home on the total amount you are willing to lose gambling. The amount might be $5, $10, or $15. No matter what happens, do not exceed this limit. If you lose, do not try to win your money back. Consider it the amount you spent to have a good time. Do not base your spending limit on time. For example, "I will play at poker for two hours." Instead, decide how much you are willing to lose: "I will play poker with $15." Once the $15 is gone, even if only an hour has passed, your session is over.

Never borrow money to gamble.

Don't gamble when it is illegal.

Don't gamble if it interferes with school or work.

Don't gamble if you are tired, depressed, or sick.

Don't gamble if it will influence the outcome of a sports event.

Don't gamble if it is prohibited by a group you belong to, like school or sports.

Don't gamble if you are recovering from other addictions.

Don't use alcohol or other drugs when gambling. These substances impair your judgment and can lead you to lose more money.

4

Gambling,
the Addiction

Anthony and his family had never entered a casino before they moved to a town near Atlantic City. They had no interest in any type of gambling at all, not even the lottery. But Atlantic City casino advertising was everywhere in their new town. Outdoor billboards, newspaper ads, junk mail, and radio and TV commercials never let Anthony's family forget that a million-dollar jackpot was waiting just for them. The casinos were so near, only minutes away, that it seemed like they were calling to Anthony's family, inviting them to a wonderful party.

Anthony's family gave in. They visited a casino. It was so easy just to drive over and play a few games. The casinos sparkled and glittered with excitement. This was the place to be! When Anthony's parents won $150 on their first night, they were even happier about their glamorous night out.

Gambling began to seem like a great way to have fun. Soon, Anthony's parents were going to the casinos every weekend. Anthony's friends talked him into sneaking into casinos after school. Even though Anthony and his friends were only 17, they got in with fake IDs.

Anthony started playing the slot machines. He especially liked the fruit machines where rows of lemons and cherries lined up for the jackpot. Anthony looked forward to playing the machines. Soon, it was all he could think about. At night, he dreamed of winning. In school, he daydreamed of what he would buy when he won big.

One day, Anthony took the $200 he had saved to buy new clothes, and instead of heading for the mall, he went to a casino. He used the money to play the machines and lost it all. Anthony realized now he would not have new clothes for at least six months. He probably would not have much money for movies either.

The Rise of Gambling

For years, most people had no access to legal gambling, and they apparently had no desire to gamble illegally. But as the legal gambling industry has expanded, more people have access to it. Some experts predict that soon, every American will live within a two-hour drive of a casino. As a result, more people are becoming addicted to gambling, according to Dr. Roger Svendsen, director of the Gambling Problems Resource Center in Minnesota.

The National Coalition Against Legalized Gambling, based in Washington, D.C., reports that in Iowa, the legalization of casinos and riverboats more than tripled the addiction problem there. In Minnesota, as 16 Indian casinos opened across the state, the number of Gamblers Anonymous groups shot up from one to 49.

Who Becomes a Compulsive Gambler?

We have seen how living near a casino can create an increase in compulsive gambling. In addition, certain people are more likely to gamble compulsively than others. The following list describes people who are more likely to gamble compulsively. Keep in mind that even if a person falls into one of these categories, it doesn't mean that person will become a compulsive gambler. On the other hand, a person can gamble compulsively and not match any of these categories.

1. **Males.** The Council on Compulsive Gambling reports that gamblers of all types are 70 percent male, and 30 percent female. Student surveys done in Minnesota during 1989, 1992, and 1995 reported the same finding. Dr. Henry Lesieur reports in "Adolescent Gambling Research: The Next Wave," a paper presented at the North American Think Tank on Youth Gambling Issues at the Harvard Medical School in 1995, that every single study he reviewed showed that males are far more likely to gamble.

   More males than females gamble and more males are likely to become compulsive gamblers. Sociologists are not yet sure why more males than females gamble. But even though females are less likely to gamble, and to gamble compulsively, they still can develop problems.

2. **Teens whose parents gamble.** If someone's parent is a problem gambler, he or she is more likely to be one as well. Some 81 percent of teens who gamble do so with their family, and 86 percent of those do so at least once a week, according to a paper titled "Children's Gambling Behavior: Familial and Social Influences," presented at the 10th National Conference on Gambling Behavior in Chicago in September 1996 by Dr. Rina Gupta and Dr. Jeffrey Derevensky, from the Department of Educational & Counseling Psychology, McGill University.

   Dr. Henry Lesieur studied children of Gamblers Anonymous members and published his findings in the *Journal of Gambling Behavior* in 1994. He found that 75 percent of problem gamblers' children reported that their first gambling experience occurred before age 11, compared to 34 percent of others. An unpublished study by Ken Winters titled "Summary of College Gambling Findings at the University of Minnesota" also found that students who have a parent with a gambling problem reported more frequent gambling of their own, whether problematic or not.

Children of problem gamblers also have higher than average use of tobacco, alcohol, and drugs and have more problems with eating disorders, especially over-eating. See Chapter Six to find out more about family gambling problems.

3. **People who live near casinos and other legalized gambling.** The exposure to more gambling opportunities seems to lead to more compulsive gambling. To be a compulsive gambler, you must gamble, and exposure to gambling increases for teens who live near casinos. For example, a 1987 study by Acuri, Lester, and Klein, published in *Adolescence,* showed that 64 percent of Atlantic City high school students had gambled in the local casinos at least once. The Casino Control Commission in New Jersey found that between 1993 and 1995, 178,000 underage gamblers were stopped at the door of a casino and another 15,000 were escorted from the building. As reported earlier, many studies have shown that when legalized gambling is allowed, more people start seeking treatment for problem gambling.

4. **High school dropouts.** Studies show that people without a high school diploma spend five times more on the lottery than do people who have a college degree. Although spending a lot of money on the lottery does not always lead to problem gambling, it does increase the potential for problems. See Chapter Seven for more about gambling and school.

5. **Video game players.** Some researchers, most notably Dr. Derevensky and Dr. Rina Gupta of McGill University,

have done studies linking obsessive use of video games to a tendency to compulsively gamble. (*Obsessive* describes an activity that totally dominates a person's actions, thoughts, or feelings.)

Video games and gambling activities have been reported to make use of similar features, most significantly, intermittent reinforcement schedules. *Intermittent schedules of reinforcement* means you never really know when you are going to win, or in the case of video games, achieve a certain goal. So, you keep on playing and playing with the belief that your win or goal will eventually happen. Some people find these schedules of reinforcement highly addictive, and so gamblers and video game players can literally play for hours and hours. Something that is addictive causes a person to be so reliant on that activity or substance that stopping is either impossible, extremely difficult, or causes severe trauma.

6. **People with attention-deficit disorder (ADD).** Attention-deficit disorder is a condition in which a person can't seem to sit still, has trouble sleeping, is easily distracted, often acts on impulse, and has difficulty paying attention. *The Addiction Letter,* December 1995, published a report of a study that strongly linked compulsive gambling to attention-deficit disorder. A team at the Brecksville, Ohio, Veterans Administration Hospital looked for symptoms of ADD in gamblers. They found that 30 to 50 percent of the gamblers they studied had ADD.

7. **Genetic inheritance.** Some scientists think that people who gamble compulsively may do so because their genes have programmed them this way or because their brain produces chemicals that cause this behavior. Biological and genetic theories of behavior are very controversial; scientists do not agree on whether the theories are valid, and many more studies are still needed.

A study reported in *American Scientist,* March/April 1996, written by Dr. David Comings and others, reports that the brain chemical dopamine and its pathways in the brain may be involved with compulsive behavior. Dopamine transmits feelings of euphoria. The scientists measured the level of this chemical in compulsive gamblers' body fluids, in particular, their spinal fluid. Their findings leads some scientists to suspect that compulsive gambling may have a biochemical cause. As research on brain function continues to grow, this theory will be tested in more depth.

This type of research is important because there are currently several different theories on what causes compulsive gambling. Some people think that compulsive gambling is a medical disease, others view it as a psychological problem, while still others view it as a moral weakness. Scientists who think compulsive gambling is a medical disease are currently doing studies that look for biochemical signs that compulsive gamblers have a different body chemistry than everyone else. Psychologists tend to explore the possibility that people gamble compulsively to cope with feelings of depression and helplessness. Other people view compulsive gambling as a character defect that could be corrected if the person just tried harder.

What the Psychiatric Community Says

A major mental health organization, The American Psychiatric Association, has identified compulsive gambling as a psychiatric illness. The American Psychiatric Association's Diagnostic and Statistical Manual of Mental Disorders (DSM) has classified gambling as an impulse control, dependence disorder. It describes pathological gambling as:

A chronic and progressive failure to resist impulses to gamble, and gambling behavior that compromises, disrupts or damages personal, family or vocational pursuits. The gambling preoccupation, urge and activity increases during periods of stress. Problems that arise as a result of the gambling lead to increased and frantic gambling. Behavioral characteristic problems include extensive indebtedness and consequent default on debts and other financial responsibility, disrupted family relationships, inattention to work and financially motivated illegal activities to pay for gambling.

The psychiatric community says that compulsive gamblers, in general, have low self-esteem. They may use gambling to compensate for feelings of inadequacy. Their poor impulse control may lead them to continue gambling even when they know it is causing severe problems. Gambling may feed their compulsive need for immediate gratification and their need to escape into fantasy. The feelings of euphoria when winning are like a drug that compulsive gamblers seek over and over. They usually don't realize that the gambling may really be a cover for extreme pain, anxiety, and depression.

How Gambling Is Similar to Substance Abuse

Gambling is a lot like smoking or drinking in that once people start, they often find it very difficult to stop. In fact, many compulsive gambling experts believe that getting hooked on gambling is very similar to getting hooked on drugs or alcohol. A new study showed that 36 percent of all people receiving treatment for compulsive gambling in Minnesota have previously received treatment for chemical dependency as well. Studies of other treatment populations show the percentage to be as high as 57 percent.

In support of these studies, many gambling experts, including Sandra Brustuen, a nationally certified gambling counselor and coordinator of a pathological gambling treatment program, have identified something called "a high prevalence of cross-addiction" between gambling and drug addiction. This means that compulsive gamblers are also likely to be alcoholics or drug abusers, while alcoholics and drug abusers have a higher-than-average tendency to become compulsive gamblers. This finding is supported by a 1994 paper, "The Emergence of Youthful Gambling and Drug Use: The Prevalence of Underage Lottery Use and the Impact of Gambling" by Dr. Howard Shaffer, Division on Addictions, Harvard Medical School, which found that many teens who use drugs also gamble.

Another expert, Dr. Richard Rosenthal, wrote in a 1992 article "Pathological Gambling," published in *Psychiatric Annuals,* that "the co-occurrence of chemical dependency and pathological gambling is frequent." *Chemical dependency* is another term for drug or alcohol addiction. Likewise, an article by Dr. Henry Lesieur published in the British Journal of Addiction in 1988 showed that the incidence of pathological gambling among a group of teen substance abusers that he studied was between 30 to 60 percent.

Co-addiction is also known as "sequential addiction," to suggest that a person might go on to develop one addiction after another. Some recovering compulsive gamblers even have a saying about it: "Drinkers put down the bottle, and pick up a deck of cards. Then they put down the deck of cards and pick up a knife and fork." In other words, the people who cite this saying believe that some people who drink too much may be able to stop their abuse of alcohol, but then they start to have a problem with gambling. If they try to stop gambling, then they may develop a problem with overeating.

Compulsive gambling is like chemical dependency in that both involve the following issues:

- **Intense preoccupation with a type of behavior:** For example, as in a person's entire social life revolving around getting drunk with friends and a person who wakes up worrying about how to get enough money to pay the dealer or the bookie.

- **Chronic, habitual behavior** that lasts over a long period of time: As in a person who has been getting drunk every weekend for six months and a person who has played cards three times a week for three months.
- **Depression, anxiety, and low-self esteem:** As in a person who is depressed after drinking too much and feels that life seems too difficult to handle and a person who feels so nervous after losing money gambling that he or she gets terrible stomach aches.
- **Denial that a problem exists** with rationalizations explaining why an apparent difficulty is not really a problem: As in a person who drinks every night but believes this is the only way to deal with life and a person who gambles every weekend but thinks that everyone else does the same thing.
- **Requiring increasing amounts of the stimulant to achieve the desired affect:** As in a person who used to drink one beer on Friday night now needs to drink three to feel the same way and a person who used to spend $5 a week on the lottery but now spends $20.
- **Gambling more or taking more drugs than intended:** As in a person who only meant to have one glass of wine but ended up drinking half a bottle and a person who only meant to spend $20 at the racetrack ending up spending $100.
- **Breakdown of family and social relationships:** As in a person whose friends start to feel uncomfortable with how much and how often the person drinks and a person whose family resents how much money is spent on gambling instead of on food.
- **Intense and uncomfortable withdrawal symptoms:** As in a person who tries to stop drinking but is unable to go even one day and a person who tries to stop gambling but feels it is impossible.

How Gambling and Substance Abuse Differ

Even though there are many similarities, there are also significant differences between gambling and chemical dependency. Gambling addiction has been found to overwhelm a person more quickly than chemical dependency. "A person with alcoholism might appear to manage drinking for 15 years before the drinking becomes an overwhelming problem, but the demise of a pathological gambler might take less than a year. Pathological gambling runs its course very quickly, especially when compared to the progression of alcoholism," writes certified gambling counselor Sandra Brustuen in *Pathological Gambling & Chemical Dependency,* a booklet produced by Project Turnaround of Minnesota. Teens can become addicted to gambling even more quickly than adults.

Gambling can usually be hidden from friends and family and kept a secret longer than a drug or alcohol problem might be. When people gamble, they don't stagger, fall down, or have slurred speech as someone who is drunk or high might do. Consequently, it may be harder for other people to notice that a person has a problem with gambling.

Compulsive gambling also tends to cause more severe financial problems than chemical dependency for many. While buying alcohol or drugs can be expensive, compulsive gambling usually involves getting into debt for thousands of dollars.

One of the biggest differences between problem gambling and drugs or alcohol problems is that the general public is far more aware of chemical dependency than it is of compulsive gambling. This is partly because the expansion of lotteries, casinos, and other gambling arenas and the related problems with compulsive gambling has happened so fast that society has not yet developed a widespread awareness of the problem.

Gambling Can Be Deadly

Chemical dependency and gambling can both be deadly. Chemical dependency can often lead to overdose and death. Compulsive gambling can cause death through crime or suicide. Dr. Roger Svendsen, director of the Minnesota Institute of Public Health, reports that suicide among compulsive gamblers is five to 10 times higher than for the rest of the population.

Many compulsive gamblers commit crimes to get money to gamble, and so endanger their lives. A survey done by the state of Minnesota in 1992 found that two-thirds of compulsive gamblers had supported their gambling through illegal activities. The survey was a study done of six state-supported pathological gambling treatment centers and looked at 1,342 compulsive gamblers.

A teen might feel suicidal if his or her compulsive gambling had progressed to a point where he/she owed hundreds or thousands of dollars to a bookie and felt there was no way to pay the money back. Sometimes, compulsive gamblers think that suicide is the only solution. If gambling has made a teen alienated from his/her parents, forced him/her to steal to support the habit, severely affected his/her grades in school, and separated him/her from friends, the teen also might feel there was no solution other than suicide. If you or someone you know is thinking about suicide due to gambling or other problems, tell a school counselor or other trusted adult or call a hot line as soon as possible. There is a lot of help available for teens who are thinking about suicide. There are ways to pay back bookies, get out of trouble, or to solve problems, even if they don't seem obvious at the time.

How to Recognize the Symptoms of Gambling That's Out of Control

If you are wondering if your gambling or the gambling someone you know is compulsive, read on. Consider whether or not you agree with the following list, and why or why not. According to the Council on Compulsive Gambling of New Jersey, you may have a problem if you have ever done any of the following:

- Gambled with lunch money
- Shoplifted because you used clothing or food money to gamble
- Chased your losses, or in other words, gambled in an attempt to get even when you lost money
- Bragged about nonexistent winnings while keeping silent about losses
- Tried to prevent friends or family from knowing about your gambling
- Cut classes to gamble
- Harmed relationships with family or friends because of your gambling
- Secretively made bets over the phone or left the house in secret to gamble
- Hid betting slips and/or lottery tickets
- Borrowed or stole from parents, siblings, other relatives, friends, employers, or loan sharks
- Sold personal property to get money to gamble

If you or someone you know has done any items on this list once or twice, there may not be a problem. But if this list feels very familiar, if you find yourself feeling uncomfortable or anxious while reading it, if you are starting to wonder about other types of behavior, or if just thinking about this issue makes you feel angry, you may want to think further about your (or someone else's) relationship to gambling. To find out more, look at the next chapter on getting help.

Are You a Compulsive Gambler?

If you answer yes to any of these questions, you may want to think about whether your gambling is getting out of control. These questions are adapted from the Council on Compulsive Gambling of New Jersey and from other organizations dedicated to helping compulsive gamblers.

1. Do you lose time from school due to gambling?
2. Have your grades dropped because of gambling?
3. Do you gamble in school?
4. Do you feel that your friends are envious of you when you win or that you get extra attention because of it?
5. Is gambling the most exciting thing you do?
6. Do one or both of your parents gamble a lot?
7. Does your life center around sports-related literature, sporting events on television, or finding out the scores/winners of sporting events?
8. Do you call sports telephone numbers or the lottery report more than twice a week?
9. Have references to gambling or gambling language increased in your conversation?
10. Do you gamble to escape worry or trouble?
11. Is your free time consumed with gambling?
12. Have your family or friends noticed a change in your behavior or personality, such as becoming irritable, impatient, or sarcastic?
13. Do arguments, disappointments, or frustrations create within you an urge to gamble?

14. Did you ever take anything that didn't belong to you or do anything illegal to finance your gambling?
15. Do you gamble until your last dollar is gone, losing even small amounts of money that you had planned to spend on other things?
16. After losing, do you feel you must return to gambling as soon as possible to win back your losses?
17. Does gambling cause you to have difficulty sleeping?
18. Have you ever thought of suicide as a way of solving your problems?

What Goes on in the Mind of a Compulsive Gambler?

When Anthony plays the slot machines, he imagines that if he just concentrates hard enough, he can control the pictures. Other compulsive gamblers think they can control the roll of the dice or the results of video poker games. People who are obsessed with the lottery often have an intense fear that their "lucky numbers" will come up on a day they don't bet, which makes them afraid not to bet every day.

Although they know better on one level, on another level, compulsive gamblers almost believe in magic. For example, they might believe that their skill or ability plays a role in the outcome of a gambling game of chance. Even when some skill is involved, as in poker or craps, luck plays a huge part in gambling, and all the more so in games of pure chance like lottery, roulette, or slot machines, where no amount of skill affects the outcome. Yet, on some level, perhaps because their *wish* to win is so strong, compulsive gamblers fail or refuse to understand this apparently simple fact. They may also believe—again, perhaps they *wish* so intensely—that they somehow *deserve* to win, and that this deserving may also affect how the cards, the dice, or the slots will fall.

Compulsive gamblers expect the "reinforcement" of winning to come at any time, so when an actual win does take place, they believe they controlled the outcome. They believe this even though the number of times they "failed to control the outcome" occurred much more frequently. Compulsive gamblers also succumb to the lure of "intermittent reinforcement." They never know when they will get reinforced (win), so they repeat the behavior over and over. For example, when people buy lottery tickets or play poker on a regular basis, they do win sometimes. When compulsive gamblers buy a lottery ticket every day, chances are that they will win something, however small or large, a few times a year. So, the wins reinforce their belief that they controlled the outcome, even though the losses occurred much more often. Sometimes they get reinforced, but most of the time they don't. The wins never make up for all the losses.

According to such experts as the National Council on Compulsive Gambling, compulsive gamblers go through three main stages.

1) The Winning Stage. At this point, the gambler has a big win, or even a few big wins. The gambler responds by feeling excited and pleased. But instead of resting for a while—enjoying the money and the victory—the compulsive gambler feels anxious, nervous, intensely excited, and perhaps also angry or vengeful. "Now is my chance to show all those people who thought I was such a loser!" These feelings push the compulsive gambler on to gamble again as soon as possible.

2) The Losing Stage. The compulsive gambler now has been gambling for some time, and although there may be some big wins, losses come more often and have wiped out all the gains. But the gambler is sure that another big win will come, and soon, because after all, he/she did win big several times before. The compulsive gambler is so sure that another big win will occur again, he/she does whatever it takes to gamble, even if that means borrowing money or selling personal possessions. It is this unwarranted optimism that gets the gambler in trouble. For even if another big win comes, the gambler has spent way more than he/she wins and is still in debt. Even so, the person goes on gambling, and goes on losing.

3) **The Desperation Stage.** This stage inevitably appears in all compulsive gamblers. In this state, compulsive gamblers think only about gambling. Their personalty may change, they may lie, borrow, and possibly steal. They may not be in control of their lives, and it may seem as if everyone is against them and that nothing is going the way it should. School and/or work may be neglected and personal relationships may fail. They may become desperate because they can't pay debts, their reputation may be ruined, life may seem hopeless, and they may even have thoughts of suicide.

Every compulsive gambler goes through these stages—it is this progression that defines the disease. Gamblers won't go through the stages in a different order, but they might go through them more than once. For example, if a compulsive gambler realized that he was getting into trouble because he was beginning to lie to his family, he might be able to pull himself together and go back to stage one from stage three. But chances are, without help, he would progress through the process again until he was no longer in control. This is when the gambler needs to look for help.

5

Recovering from Compulsive Gambling

Mike saw a flyer about a Gambler's Anonymous meeting at a community center near his home. He decided that he had to try to stop gambling, and this seemed like a good way to start. His plan was to ask his dad to come with him. That evening, he waited up until his dad came home from a poker game. Mike knew he was taking a risk that his dad would be furious at this idea, but it was a risk he felt was well worth taking. As soon as his dad came in the front door, Mike asked, "Dad, will you come to a Gambler's Anonymous meeting with me tomorrow?" Mike's dad slammed the door behind him and yelled, "Now what would I want to do a thing like that for?" He stomped off to his room and went to bed. The next morning, however, he pulled Mike aside at breakfast and told him that if it was important to Mike, he'd go. Mike was thrilled that his plan had worked. For once, it seemed like he was doing the right thing. The next night, as he walked to the meeting with his dad in the dark evening, he felt a combination of apprehension and hope. He wasn't sure if he and his dad would be able to do what they had to do. But as he looked up at the brightly lit windows inside the community center basement, and saw other people walking inside, he was filled with inspiration.

There are many ways for teens to overcome a gambling addiction. Many people have found that getting treatment from a group such as Gamblers Anonymous or other gambling treatment organization is a good way to recover. Gamblers Anonymous is an international organization that was the result of a chance meeting between two men in January 1957. These men had a history of trouble because of their obsession with gambling. They began to meet regularly to help each other. As the months passed, they discovered that neither had returned to gambling. They concluded from their discussions that in order to prevent a relapse, it was necessary to bring about certain character changes within themselves. In order to accomplish this, they used for a guide certain principles that had been used by thousands of people who were recovering from other addictions like alcoholism. These principles are called 12-step programs because they follow a set 12 rules to guide followers through the recovery process.

The founders wanted to bring their message of hope to other compulsive gamblers. The first group meeting of Gamblers Anonymous was held on Friday, September 13, 1957, in Los Angeles. Since that time, the group has grown steadily, and Gamblers Anonymous groups are flourishing throughout the world.

The only requirement for membership is a desire to stop gambling. There are no dues or fees for Gamblers Anonymous membership. The group is self-supporting through member contributions. Its primary purpose is to stop compulsive gambling. In some areas, there are special groups for teens.

If you think you need help, or if you know someone who does, you might want to check out the list of hot lines in the back of this book. The yellow pages of your telephone book are also a good place to find gambling treatment centers or chapters of Gamblers Anonymous in your area. You may also want to confide in a friend, parent, trusted teacher, school counselor, coach, or clergy member either before or after calling.

When a person calls to get help from a hot line, there are two possible services offered. There is usually no way to tell which kind of service is being offered until after you make the phone call. A simple hot line aims to tell the person where to go for help. For example, the person may be referred to the nearest Gambler's Anonymous meeting or to a hospital-based treatment program. This kind of hot line does not offer advice over the phone.

In contrast, a helpline will offer on-the-spot suggestions for help. The person on the other end of the line will try to determine the extent of the problem and whether a crisis is occurring. The helper will try to calm down the caller if the caller is upset. The helper will try to find out if a suicide or homicide is about to occur; if so, appropriate action will be recommended. In some areas, telephone counseling for a fee may also be available.

Sometimes, simply moving away to a new community can help a teen recover. It eases the recovery process to get away from others who gamble or from a community in which gambling is prevalent. However, teens don't usually have control over where they will live, so this option is not always available.

Other times, teens recover from gambling because they have a spiritual or religious awakening, which helps them see life in a new way. The feelings of hope and joy they feel from their connection to God and their religion can be enough to help them escape the stranglehold of gambling.

Another possible way a teen gambler can be helped is if a new person in his or her life serves as a role model and helps the teen stop gambling.

Be aware that recovering from compulsive gambling can cause physical withdrawal symptoms such as stomach problems, nausea, headaches, back problems, insomnia, and stress. These are normal and will disappear as recovery continues. A treatment counselor can offer advice on what to do about them.

Compulsive gambling experts say that it may cost thousands of dollars to treat each person addicted to gambling. The costs can range from $13,000 to $50,000 per person. This is obviously very expensive, so who pays? Sometimes families pay out of their own pocket. Sometimes a state offers free help through a gambling treatment program.

It is possible for a person to recover from compulsive gambling without the help of a professional. It isn't easy, but it is worth trying.

The first step is to make a commitment to stop gambling completely. The first few days and weeks are the hardest. Since compulsive gambling is a disorder of impulse control, it will be difficult to stop the impulses that compel a person to gamble. As time goes by, it becomes easier to stay away from gambling activities.

During this time, it is a good idea for the person to get involved in things to do which are totally different than gambling. Some suggestions include starting an exercise or weight-training program, playing basketball or other active sports, and really getting into studying for school classes. Other ideas include volunteering for a club at school, reading some new books, or offering to help elderly neighbors.

People who are trying to stop gambling may have to work on improving their self-esteem as well. Making a list of all the good things a person has done and is feeling is a helpful strategy. Initiating and developing a relationship with an adult who cares will make the teen feel better too.

Getting Treatment

The feelings a teen has when deciding whether or not to get counseling for compulsive gambling may be difficult to handle. It will be hard to face life without gambling; the teen may have been dealing with life's problems by avoiding schoolwork and other responsibilities. It will feel similar to what an alcoholic feels when he or she decides to give up drinking. Giving up dice, cards, and lottery tickets is like having a drug taken away.

Individual Counseling

When a teen calls a hot line, he or she often will be encouraged to sign up for individual counseling and group counseling. The individual counseling will help the teen deal with the situation, and the counselor will offer concrete solutions to the problems that may have felt hopeless. A counselor will conduct psychological tests to determine the severity of the problem and to decide the best course of treatment. The teen will be helped to form a payment plan to pay back the people who are owed money, whether it was borrowed or stolen. Debt management and financial management skills will be taught. The counselor will also teach what are called "cognitive interventions." These are ways to control the irrational thinking, illusions of control, and automatic thoughts that are part of the gambling addiction. Training in problem solving, assertiveness, and relapse prevention are all helpful as well.

Group Counseling

The group counseling will help teens deal with emotions and feelings. Everyone in the group will be urged to talk openly and honestly about the details of their compulsive gambling. Working together, the group will encourage everyone to admit their problem and will help the members understand their problem.

Although some states have separate meetings for teens, many group meetings combine all age groups. As the awareness of teen gambling grows, most likely more states will recognize the need for separate teen meetings. These separate meetings may make it easier for teens to recover.

During the time of treatment, teens will be advised to stop gambling completely. This will include not even entering free sweepstakes or the Publisher's Clearinghouse type offers. Total abstinence is the only way to beat compulsive gambling. Skills to help teens stop gambling will be taught. "Homework" may be assigned to play a competitive game without betting, such as cards, pool, or even checkers. Another assignment may be to watch sports events without betting. Relaxation techniques will be taught, as these can help relieve the stress and tension that were relieved by gambling before.

During treatment, it may be discussed whether to take one of the new drugs being developed to help compulsive gamblers. These drugs are controversial and not universally accepted as a good option. They may, however, render the gambling urges less intense, giving the patient more ability to resist acting on gambling impulses. The drugs do have some side effects, including insomnia and mild stomach upset. Only one's doctor can decide if they are appropriate for a given individual.

Admitting to being hooked on gambling may cause a teen to feel a high degree of shame. Self-esteem may suffer. Self-esteem workshops will help relieve these feelings. Making lists of accomplishments and positive attributes helps teen compulsive gamblers see that they are good, worthy people. Making plans for a new life without gambling helps boost self-esteem a lot, too. Career plans, community work, and regular fitness programs are high on the list of activities that help teens recover.

One of the greatest sources of gratification is channeling the competitive spirit you have into competing for good grades instead of gambling. Doing well in school has lifelong rewards, both short- and long-term, that far out-weigh any that gambling can offer.

Hot Lines and Crime

Teens may be afraid to call a hot line about their compulsive gambling, especially if they have committed an illegal act like robbery to get money to gamble. Be assured that gambling hot lines are totally confidential and never report anyone to the police. Whatever the situation, however frightening it is, the person at the end of the line can help.

Teen Gamblers and the Law

A teen may want to consider contacting the police if illegal activities are involved. He or she should be aware, however, that sometimes law enforcement officials and gambling recovery experts disagree about how to handle situations in which teen gamblers have committed crimes or are involved with a bookie who is threatening them. For example, if someone went to the police and told them he could not pay his bookie and the bookie was threatening to kill him, the police would probably tell the teen not to pay the bookie anything because he is conducting illegal business. The police would then arrest the bookie and prosecute him. Most likely, they would not arrest the teen gambler.

However, gambling recovery experts point out that this may take care of the problem in the short term, but the teen will still be a compulsive gambler. The real problem will not have been solved. Therefore, they recommend that, instead of going to the police and having the bookie arrested, the teen gambler tell the bookie that he is in treatment and that he will pay him in installments. "Most bookies will respect the fact that a teen is in treatment for compulsive gambling," said Ed Looney, director of the Council on Compulsive Gambling, in a telephone inter-view.

Treatment also usually requires that teen gamblers face up to any people they have victimized. For example, if a teen broke into a house and stole money to gamble, the teen would be encouraged to meet with the homeowner and promise to make restitution, or pay back, all of the stolen money. This is the only sure way to be cured of the compulsion to gamble. Even if it takes $10 a month for 10 years to pay, most likely the person will accept the arrangement. "Very rarely does the person say no and turn the teen over to the police," says Ed Looney. However, if this does happen, it still is part of the recovery process. Courts and judges look very favorably on compulsive gamblers who have committed themselves to treatment and so are more likely to go easier on them than on a teen gambler who had been arrested but had not gotten involved in counseling.

Be aware that these actions should never be attempted without the advice of a Gamblers Anonymous or other expert. First contact them. In some cases, they may advise a teen to hire an attorney, depending on the situation.

6

Gambling and
the Family

One of the main reasons Dave found it easy to stop playing poker was because no one in his family gambles, at least not very much. His grandmother does play mah jong, a game of Chinese origin played with tiles that look like dominoes. The tiles are marked with different designs and players try to collect certain combinations. Dave's grandmother and her friends play every Friday night but limit their bets to $20 a night. Dave's aunt visits Atlantic City once in a while to vacation and gamble in the casinos. But Dave's parents don't gamble at all.

Sam's parents, who have always gambled recreationally, told him he could have a big party for his 16th birthday. At first, Sam wanted the theme to be a costume party, because his birthday is around Halloween. Then he considered having a sports party at the gym. But the idea he settled on was a casino party. He set up a table at his front door, where each guest was given $1,000 worth of play money. Then his friends could go to different areas of his house, which were set up with a blackjack table, a roulette wheel, a poker game, a dice game, and a pretend racehorse game. The guests bet their play money on the games, and at the end of the party, Sam offered a CD to the person who won the most money. Two of his friends nearly tied for top dollar, and they started pushing each other and arguing over who should get the CD.

One night when Andrea had finished her homework, she turned on her computer and went online. The chat room she usually visited was boring, though. The kids she usually traded messages with weren't there. She clicked on the bookmark for her favorite places and visited the web sites of her favorite music groups. One of them had an ad for an online casino. Even though Andrea doesn't like gambling, she was curious about this, so she clicked on the ad. The site first asked her if she was over 18 before she went any further. Andrea is only 15. She couldn't decide whether to lie or not.

Mike's parents have always held Friday night poker games at their house, and Mike liked to stand around and watch. He was fascinated with the money changing hands and the big piles of coins heaped on the table. By the age of 12, Mike was sitting at the table, playing with his parents. Later on, Mike's father took him for walks down to the corner store after dinner to buy lottery tickets. Then, Mike's father took him to the racetrack. Mike's father would let him bet $2 to show or place, and his father would bet $10 or $20. Mike fondly remembers those evening walks and racetrack experiences as the best times he ever spent with his father. He feels sad that the gambling that brought him and his father together is now creating real problems for them both, although the Gamblers Anonymous meetings are helping.

Most teens learn to gamble from someone in the family. Maybe a father invites his son or daughter along with him to buy a lottery ticket every Sunday. Maybe grandparents include the grandchildren in a fun game of poker for pennies every Friday night. Perhaps a mother plays bingo at church. If a teen's parents are just social gamblers, then there probably will not be a long-term problem resulting from a teen being exposed to gambling. A teen may still get hooked on gambling even if his or her parents are not gamblers. But if one or both of a teen's parents are problem or compulsive gamblers, the teen is at greater risk.

Sam's parents let him have the casino party because they thought it sounded like a fun idea. They, like many parents, think that in today's dangerous world, teens could be involved with a lot worse than pretend, or even real, gambling. To them, gambling is not as dangerous as drugs, alcohol, or unsafe sex. Neither Sam nor his parents realized, though, that some of Sam's friends take gambling very seriously. In fact, the two guys who were fighting over the CD were known to bet with bookies. Sam's father finally calmed the two guys down by promising to give them both a CD. Sam and his family sort of wished they hadn't promoted gambling at their party. Sam was sad for another reason. Two of his friend's parents wouldn't let them come to the party because their parents didn't approve of even pretend gambling for teens.

Andrea's parents had no idea she was even considering using a gambling site on the Internet. They were downstairs watching television. Andrea decided not to lie about her age, and clicked on the *Sports Illustrated* site instead. Andrea's experience helps show why some government officials are concerned about online gambling—there are few ways to keep teens from gambling in their own bedrooms. Internet gambling is the only form of gambling that can offer full access to anyone who has a computer, modem, phone line, and credit card. There are already hundreds of wagering sites, which offer unprecedented availability and the lure of anonymity. Even though many companies require application forms and cash deposits to protect against underage gambling, many teens are getting involved.

Mike's family life was unhappy. His parents were always fighting. If Mike had a smile on his face, his father would say, "Why are you so happy?". . . if his father was around, that is. The family dynamics when a parent is a compulsive gambler are painful, because every compulsive gambler negatively affects other people. It's hard for teens in these situations to make sense of what is happening, but if you think one of your parents is a compulsive gambler, there are ways for you to cope.

Family Problems and Gambling

Teens in families where there is a compulsive gambler may try desperately to "fix" the problems in their environment. Mike tries to intervene when his parents are fighting about his father's gambling debts, but his father just yells at him and his mother cries. Mike feels like it's his fault there are problems, even though he can't really figure out why that would be. His parents make so many promises that they never keep that he has stopped believing anything they say.

Sometimes Mike becomes a scapegoat. If his father has lost a lot of money that day, and his mother is out working, Mike's dad will take it out on him. He'll scream at Mike to do the laundry or make dinner. He'll make Mike stay in his room all night without using the phone or visiting friends. It doesn't really matter anyway. Mike long ago lost most of his friends. When friends were still coming over to his house, they were often exposed to many of his family's problems. For example, Mike was embarrassed that his dad was often sleeping on the couch after having been up all night at a casino. The house was often a mess, and Mike didn't want friends to see this.

Mike often ends up doing chores his parents have neglected. Most of the time, he doesn't mind, because he knows how hard his mother works and how troubled his father is. But what he really wants to do is make more money gambling. Mike thinks that if he gets more money through gambling, then the family's problems will be solved.

Signs That a Parent May Have a Problem with Compulsive Gambling

Are you wondering if one of your parents may be a compulsive gambler? You may feel confused because you sense something is wrong but you are not sure what it is. Compulsive gambling is often hard to identify. An alcoholic parent may have more obvious symptoms, like slurred speech or drunken behavior, but how would a family member know if someone had a secret credit line with a bookie?

If a parent has a job but often does not go, or keeps losing jobs, there may be a problem. If a parent is involved with substance abuse, that is enough to be concerned.

There may be many phone calls, even harassment, by creditors to whom the parents owe money for household bills. Or bookies to whom the parent owes money may call. Parents may fight over the fact that money was gambled away so there is not enough to pay bills. Gambling may cause divorce and leave families in debt. The Illinois Council on Compulsive Gambling surveyed 200 compulsive gamblers and found that 16 percent were divorced due to their gambling, and another 10 percent had separated.

Parents may have insomnia, depression, and mistrust of each other and everyone in the family. There may be spouse abuse and/or substance abuse. Calls to women's crisis centers rise when casinos enter a community. Teens may feel neglected by parents who are gamblers. They, too, may become depressed and even suicidal.

What to Do If Parents, Siblings, or Friends Gamble a Lot

If you know someone who gambles a lot, you are sure to have feelings about the person's activities. Perhaps you are worried that a brother will gamble away the money he is supposed to be saving for college. Or a friend may be drifting away from your relationship because of her involvement in gambling, and you wish the two of you were closer. A parent's gambling activities may be causing you concern, especially if there is a lot of tension in the household. Here is what you can do if you want to try to talk to friends or family about their gambling. This advice is adapted from work done by Dr. Roger Svendsen and Tom Griffin of the Gambling Problem Resource Center in Minnesota. They advise that you choose a good, quiet time to talk when neither the person nor yourself is under the influence of any drugs or alcohol.

1. Tell the person that you care about him or her and that you feel concerned about the way you see him or her acting. Say things like:
   - "I love you and Mom and am worried that you gamble too much."
   - "I love you and don't want you to get in trouble."
   - "As a good friend I'm concerned, because you are doing something that could cause a problem for you."
2. Tell the person exactly what he or she has done that concerns you. Say things like:
   - "You haven't paid the telephone bill, and they called to say the phone will be turned off."

- "You borrowed money from me and haven't paid me back."
- "You aren't home for dinner, and I go to sleep without seeing you."

3. After you tell the person that you care, how you feel and what you've seen, it's important to be willing to listen to what he or she says. The person may:
   - Say nothing, because he or she may not be ready to talk with you.
   - Become angry and say that these things are none of your business.
   - Thank you and offer to consider making changes in his or her behavior.
   - Suddenly say disturbing things that you weren't prepared to hear. The person may reveal the deep extent of his or her problem, which may be more troubling than you suspected.
4. Tell the person what you would like to see him or her do. This may include:
   - Setting limits in the future.
   - Talking to another person, either a trusted friend, relative, or religious leader.
   - Calling a compulsive gambling hotline.
   - Visiting and joining Gamblers Anonymous.
5. Tell the person what you are willing or able to do or help. This may include:
   - Being available to talk again.
   - Assisting in finding help. However, help should not include lending money to a gambler.

Coping with Anger If a Parent Is a Compulsive Gambler

What if your father or mother gambles away family money meant for food, clothing, or education? If this happens, you are likely to feel a lot of anger. You may find it helpful to attend meetings of Gam-Anon. This is a group for people who are not gamblers themselves but who have been affected by compulsive gamblers, including the children, wives, husbands, relatives, and close friends of gamblers. There are Gam-Anon groups in most large cities. See the resource section at the end of the book on how to contact them. If there are no groups in your area, you may want to start your own. People at Gam-Anon headquarters can tell you how to do this.

Gam-Anon holds talk sessions in which everyone is free to vent their feelings. The groups help members seek solutions for living with the problems caused by compulsive gamblers. Going on the theory that no one can change another person, especially a compulsive gambling parent, Gam-Anon focuses on helping its members change their own lives. They advise members to try to be understanding of the gambling member in the home. Members are shown that they can help themselves by getting to know other people who are living with compulsive gamblers. Sometimes, a problem gambler may even join Gamblers Anonymous, as a result of one or more family members belonging to Gam-Anon. Gam-Anon is not directly affiliated with Gamblers Anonymous, though the two groups do cooperate.

If you do decide to take action, such as attending a Gam-Anon meeting, don't expect things to change right away. The goal is for the participants to change their own feelings, not to change the behavior of the person who is having problems with gambling. Any sort of change like this takes time, effort, and a large amount of patience.

7

Gambling at School and in the Community

The guest speaker asked the class, "Do any of you feel like you must gamble and can't stop? Have you ever stolen money from your parents to gamble? Do you bet on sports with a bookie? Don't answer me, just think about it." Mike secretly answered yes to himself, then pulled his desk a little farther to the back of his homeroom. Most of the guys knew Mike liked to gamble. Would they expose him? He felt like he needed to run out of the room, but his teacher was standing in front of the door.

It was Addiction Awareness Week at Mike's school, and the students had heard several lectures about drugs, alcohol, and tobacco. Mike already knew those things were addictive. But this gambling talk was something new. No one ever had ever told him that gambling could be addictive.

Mike wondered if he was addicted to gambling. He thought about how he bought a lottery ticket at the corner store every morning on the way to school. Even though he is too young to legally buy lottery tickets, the man behind the counter never questioned him for being underage. He thought about the dice in his pocket, ready for a few games of see-low after lunch in the cafeteria. The teachers knew the kids were playing, but they didn't seem to care. Mostly Mike thought about the $500 he owed the bookie this week for sports bets. Mike didn't have the money this time. And he heard if you didn't pay the bookie, you might end up in the hospital, or worse.

Just then, the speaker said, "If you think you have a problem with gambling, call this 800 number. We'll help you." And then the thing that Mike feared the most, happened. Scott, always a big mouth, called out, "Hey, will you pay off Mike's bookie for him?" Everyone laughed and turned around to look at Mike. He wished he could run out of the room and never go back.

Mike did eventually call the 800 number and got help. He was lucky—many teens that are trapped in a gambling web don't realize they can get help. Ed Looney, executive director of the New Jersey Council on Compulsive Gambling, visits schools to tell students about gambling. He tells them true stories about teens who are too scared to go to school because they can't pay back their bookies who are fellow students.

Looney knows lots of stories, but there are many others that no one knows about. What about the boy who steals sandwiches from the school cafeteria so he can bet his lunch money? Or the kids who gamble after school out on the sidewalk? One gambling game that is gaining popularity in schools is called see-low. Teens use three dice, which they rub against the arch of their sneakers for luck, and then cast them. Bets can go up to $5 a game. To get a "see-low" means you get a four-five-six combination on the dice. A one-two-three is an automatic loss called "aced."

See-low is a street variation on craps. It has been around for a long time but is newly popular in high schools. Sometimes there are hundreds of dollars riding on a single roll.

Here is an example of a school that wanted its students to know more about gambling. In 1993, the Woodbridge Township School District was the first in New Jersey to conduct a program for compulsive gamblers. Gambling experts spoke to students and their parents and conducted training sessions with teachers. The school distributed book covers that were printed with 10 signs to identify teen compulsive gamblers and an 800 number. The school administration set up a policy that bars all gambling on school property and at school-sponsored events. When gambling is found on school grounds, students can face disciplinary action. The purpose of the policy is not to punish teens but to instruct and help them. Students with gambling problems are encouraged to contact a school counselor. While the gambling policy can't stop all students from gambling, it does help make students realize that if they or any of their friends have a problem, they have some place to turn for help.

Do kids gamble at your school? Is anyone telling them not to? Do you think students should be allowed to gamble in your school? Why or why not? Most school handbooks these days warn about alcohol, drugs, and sexual harassment, but never mention gambling.

But many gambling experts say schools should forbid student gambling on school grounds. For example, card playing might be allowed in the cafeteria, but students would not be allowed to gamble on the outcome. School policies on gambling should describe what constitutes gambling, conditions under which a policy applies, and the responsibilities of staff for implementing what actions taken against students who do. If you are interested in forming a committee to help establish a gambling policy at your school, talk to a guidance counselor, a teacher, or the principal.

Another topic to consider for your school policy is whether gambling games should be used as fund-raisers. Most schools and youth groups don't realize that raffles are a form of gambling. Raffles, bingo, and school lotteries are common school fund-raisers. Some schools have casino nights for parents. Many gambling experts think that with these activities, students are receiving the message that gambling is acceptable and harmless for teens. If you'd like to change the type of fund-raisers your school has, you can suggest alternative forms of fund-raising for your school, such as bake sales, car washes, flea markets, or craft fairs.

What's the difference between these fund-raisers and raffles or bingo? When you pay money for a car wash, cupcake, or used book, you are getting something tangible in return. You are buying more than just a chance at winning.

If you go on to college, you may find that gambling is even more prevalent there than in high school. *Sports Illustrated* ran a three-part series in April, May, and June 1995 whose author commented, "Gambling is the dirty little secret on college campuses, where it's rampant and prospering." The article went on to describe how easy it is for students to bet with a bookie, become consumed with wagering, and get over their heads in debt.

Dealing with Peer Pressure to Bet

Since dice games, card games, and sports betting were popular at Dave's school, he felt a lot of pressure to participate. He joined in several times. He first played for pennies, then nickels, then dollars. Dave realized he felt uncomfortable with either outcome, winning or losing. If he lost his own money, he felt cheated, and if he won his friend's money, he felt guilty.

One way Dave could get out of these uncomfortable situations is to find new friends who aren't into gambling. But he doesn't want to do that. He likes his friends too much, and there isn't anyone else he wants to hang with. Teens in this position can still keep their friends, even if the friends are gambling and they aren't, but there may be difficulties.

Friends who gamble may ask to borrow money frequently. They may pay it back, but it is more likely that they won't. It's a good idea to refuse to lend money to anyone. Teens can tell friends who ask that they don't lend money. This avoids many problems that can result from lending, such as anger and resentment.

In addition, it's better not to carry a lot of cash to school. If teens don't have much money to lend, no one can be mad at them for not lending it. If a teen has a wad of bills in his pocket, however, friends who need money for whatever reason will pressure him for it.

Another strategy to avoid actually gambling is to watch the games but not participate. Although there will be pressure to join in, teens can stand their ground, and eventually the others will stop asking. However, there are some drawbacks to standing around watching dice and card games. If a disagreement or argument arises over rules, money, or cheating, the friends who were gambling may demand that someone referee the situation. This can be very uncomfortable for anyone who is just a spectator.

If you have a friend who is gambling a lot, you might want to tell him or her that you are concerned that he or she is doing something that could cause a problem for him or her. You might want to encourage your friend to call a compulsive gambling hot line or talk to a trusted school counselor. Tell the friend that you are available for talking and for finding help but that you will not lend him or her money.

Gambling and Teen Crime

Some teens who are problem gamblers commit crimes to get money to gamble because they have no other way to get money. Their friends have stopped lending to them, their parents won't give it to them, and they've lost whatever they may have saved or earned. In this way, teens are like adults who are compulsive gamblers. For people in both age groups, crime and problem gambling go hand-in-hand.

U.S. News & World Reports published an article on January 15, 1996, analyzing crime and gambling. The article showed that crime rates are higher in places with gambling. A computer analysis showed that towns with casinos experienced an upsurge of crime at the same time crime was dropping for the nation as a whole. The places that had gotten new casinos the year before saw their crime jump the most. There were 1,092 incidents of crime per 10,000 people in 1994 in places with casinos, compared with 593 per 10,000 people for other places in the country. Yet, according to the article, people are not being arrested for illegal gambling. The article said that law-enforcement agencies have concentrated their resources on fighting illegal drugs, not on fighting gambling. In 1960, 123,000 people were arrested for illegal gambling—3 percent of all arrests nationwide. In 1996, only 15,000 people were arrested for illegal gambling, only 1 percent of all arrests.

The National Council on Compulsive Gambling has found that 65 percent of all gamblers treated have committed a crime. In a Gambling Treatment Outcome Study of treatment effectiveness in Minnesota, it was found that one in five clients of gambling treatment centers reported that his/her legal status was either that of being on parole or on probation as a result of gambling-related problems. At least 10 percent of the clients had been arrested for a gambling-related offense in the six months prior to treatment.

Sometimes, after losing an entire paycheck on gambling, gamblers may commit a crime to get money to pay their bills. They may pawn expensive jewelry or other items to fund their gambling, then tell police the item was stolen. Police around casinos notice an increase in these types of false reports.

There is a long list of crimes that adults and teens commit to get money to gamble when their legal avenues to fund gambling run out. Forging checks and committing loan fraud are common. Teens will often steal cash, checks, and credit cards from their parents and others. Embezzling and employee theft, both of which involve taking money from employers, are also common. Robbery is common, as well as fencing (or selling) the stolen goods. Pimping and prostitution are also common. Some problem gamblers become bookies or run con games.

Gamblers are also often the target of crimes. A thief who sees them win big may follow them home and steal their winnings.

About Bookmakers

An article in the October 1996 issue of *Chicago* magazine tells of a family man named Joe who secretly ran a bookie business with as many as 40 clients. He was eventually arrested, but because of his lack of a previous record was given probation and a small fine. Joe could be the father of someone you know. Although Joe didn't get jail time, becoming a bookie or betting with one is far from safe. Betting with a bookie may help fuel organized crime, including gun trafficking, drugs, and mob violence. When you bet with bookies, that money may be used to sell drugs in your neighborhood, to purchase weapons that will kill innocent people, and to fund loan-sharking activities.

Here is what might happen if someone bets with a bookie. Suppose Mike started with a $25 bet on a football game. Suppose his team loses, so he loses the money. The bookmaker will probably allow Mike to try to make up his debt by betting again the next week, so that his winnings can cover the previous week's losses. Eventually, however, Mike may lose more money, so that he needs to make larger bets to cover his losses. Within a short time, Mike and others can lose hundreds of dollars.

Bookies who deal with teens believe that parents will step in and pay the bill if the teen can't. They threaten and pressure kids to pay, and they also act as high-pressure salespeople to try to keep teens betting. They might come to the teen's house and show pictures of people whose legs they've broken.

For example, according to an Associated Press report of November 9, 1996, a student who says he placed bets for five Boston College football players had to be hospitalized after he was attacked with a two-by-four by a New York bookmaker. His father told the *Boston Globe* that the student owed the bookie $4,000. To save their son from further harm, the parents made four weekly payments of $1,000 to a man they met outside a bar. But compulsive gambling experts warn parents that bailing out a teen who is a pathological gambler does not get to the source of the problem.

These days, Dave's lucky shirt and lucky hat are pushed to the back of his closet. Dave doesn't have much interest in them anymore since he stopped gambling for fun. His friends still play poker however. They play less frequently, though, since they are all now much more into studying to get into a good college. Dave took his SATs recently and did very well. He thinks he might want to major in mathematics, or maybe chemistry.

Sam sold his book, "How to Dream Your Lucky Numbers," at a garage sale held by his family. An elderly man bought it for 50 cents. Sam hoped the man wouldn't be angry with him when he discovered the book didn't work.

Sam is also busy planning his next Oscar pool. He is sure that Will Smith or Ben Affleck will win something this year.

Andrea still doesn't gamble at all, but she found out she does like to play blackjack just for fun. She plays it with her cousin Brandon, who isn't interested in chase cards any more. Now, when they go to the candy store together, instead of buying sports cards in the hopes that a chase card will be inside, Brandon buys the kind of candy that is so sour that it tastes like it isn't even safe to eat. Andrea thinks maybe buying chase cards wasn't so bad compared to the crazy candies.

Mike and his dad enjoyed their first Gambler's Anonymous meeting. They were surprised how many people attended. One of their neighbors was even there. Everyone had to stand up and tell a little about themselves and what their particular problem was. Then a few men went to the front of the room and told stories about how they had severe gambling problems and how they had overcome them. Everyone applauded at the end of their stories. Mike even felt tears come to eyes. He hoped that he and his father would be able to stand up proud one day and tell how they were able to stop gambling. It was not going to be easy. But he felt sure that it would one day be reality.

Gambling is here to stay in our society, that's for sure. In a few years, you will grow from a teen into an adult, and all types of gambling will be legal for you to enjoy. Now that you have read this book, you understand more about gambling than most people. You will be able to make decisions about gambling based on the knowledge you have gained—responsible decisions that are right for you and your life.

8

Where to
Find Help

Web Sites

The Internet is a good place to look for information and resources. Here are web sites that offer information and/or help to those with gambling problems.

Council on Compulsive Gambling of New Jersey
http://www.800gambler.org

Gamblers Anonymous
www.gamblersanonymous.org

Gamblers Book Club
http://www.gamblersbook.com/index.htm
Sells books on how to gamble as well as books about compulsive gambling; can also be reached at 1-800-522-1777.

National Council on Problem Gambling
http://www.ncpgambling.org

North American Training Institute (a division of the
Minnesota Council on Compulsive Gambling, Inc.)
http://www.nati.org

Gambling Hot Lines and Agencies

The Council on Compulsive Gambling of New Jersey, Inc.
800-GAMBLER
(800-426-2537)

Gam-Anon I.S.O.
P.O. Box 157
Whitestone, NY 11357
(718) 352-1671
For families and friend of problem gamblers

Minnesota Compulsive Gambling Hotline
800-437-3641
Run by the Minnesota Institute of Public Health, Gambling
Problems Resource Center, Department of Human Services

National Coalition AGAINST Legalized Gambling
110 Maryland Avenue, NE
Washington DC 20002
800-664-2680
A grassroots organization dedicated to stopping the spread
of legalized gambling through information and education

National Council on Problem Gambling
800-522-4700

Gamblers Anonymous

Gamblers Anonymous
International Service Office
P.O. Box 17173
Los Angeles, CA 90017
(213) 386-8789
Fax (213) 386-0030
www.gamblersanonymous.org
Includes a listing of local meetings and contacts
For people with gambling problems

Below are local phone numbers for chapters of Gamblers Anonymous. If you do not find one near you, call the headquarters listed above or consult your local phone book or their web site. The phone numbers may change, so if you call a number that is not correct, call the headquarters listed above.

Alabama
Birmingham (205) 290-8803

Arizona
Phoenix (602) 266-9784

California
Los Angeles (310) 478-2121
Sacramento (916) 447-5588
San Diego (619) 239-2911
San Francisco (800) 287-8670
San Jose (800) 287-8670

Canada
Calgary, Alberta (403) 237-0654
Montreal, Quebec (514) 484-6666
Toronto, Ontario (416) 366-7613
Vancouver, British Columbia (604) 685-5510
Windsor, Ontario (519) 977-9620

Colorado
Denver (303) 754-7119

Connecticut
statewide (203) 777-5585

Delaware
statewide (302) 984-2277

District of Columbia
Washington, DC (301) 961-1313

Florida
Broward/Palm Beach (305) 537-1367
Miami (305) 447-2696
Orlando (407) 236-9206
Sarasota (941) 957-7928
Tampa (813) 877-0969
Central Florida hot line (800) 397-9843

Georgia
Atlanta (404) 237-7281

Illinois
Chicago (312) 346-1588

Indiana
Indianapolis (317) 382-4950

Kansas
statewide (816) 346-9230

Kentucky
Lexington (606) 277-8236
Louisville (502) 561-5665

Louisiana
New Orleans (504) 836-4543

Maryland
Baltimore (410) 377-3889

Massachusetts
Boston (617) 338-6020
Springfield (413) 746-7192

Michigan
statewide (313) 535-3086

Minnesota
Minneapolis (612) 922-3956

Mississippi
statewide (601) 864-0442

Missouri
St. Louis (314) 647-1111

Montana
Billings (406) 860-8287
Butte (406) 496-6100
Helena (406) 449-8268

Nebraska
Lincoln (402) 473-7933
Omaha (402) 978-7557

Nevada
Las Vegas (702) 385-7732
Reno (702) 356-8070
South Lake Tahoe (916) 573-2423

New Hampshire
statewide (603) 644-8097

New Jersey
statewide (908) 756-1171
(800) 425-4837
(609) 429-6516

New Mexico
Albuquerque (505) 260-7272
Santa Fe (505) 984-7277

New York
Albany (518) 463-2586
Long Island (516) 586-7171
New York City (212) 903-4400
Syracuse (315) 458-0085

North Carolina
statewide (800) 313-0170

Ohio
Cincinnati (513) 244-9779
Cleveland (216) 771-2248
Columbus (614) 262-9022
Toledo (419) 327-9514
Youngstown (216) 793-6893

Oklahoma
Oklahoma City (405) 525-2026
Tulsa (918) 669-6999

Oregon
Portland (503) 233-5888

Pennsylvania
Philadelphia (215) 468-1991
Pittsburgh (412) 281-7484

Rhode Island
statewide (401) 553-1441

South Carolina
statewide (800) 313-0170

South Dakota
statewide (605) 339-4357

Tennessee
Knoxville (615) 588-4911
Memphis (901) 371-4083
Nashville (615) 254-6454

Texas
Dallas (214) 890-0005
Houston (713) 684-6654

Utah
Salt Lake City (801) 566-3390

Virginia
Roanoke (540) 989-0974

Washington
Seattle (206) 361-8413
Vancouver (360) 896-9602
Tacoma (253) 925-3203

West Virginia
Wheeling (304) 234-9799

Wisconsin
statewide (414) 299-0901
Green Bay (414) 469-9957

For Further Reading

Books

Davis, Bertha. *Gambling in America: A Growth Industry.* New York: Franklin Watts, 1992.

Dolan, Edward F. *Teenagers and Compulsive Gambling.* New York: Franklin Watts, 1994.

Haddock, Patricia. *Teens and Gambling: Who Wins? (Issues in Focus).* Springfield, New Jersey: Enslow Pub., 1996.

Haubrich-Casperson, Jane. *Coping with Teen Gambling.* New York: Rosen Pub. Group, 1993.

Hjelmeland, Andy. *Legalized Gambling: Curse or Salvation?* Minneapolis, Minn.: Lerner, 1998.

Hyde, Margaret O. *Gambling: Winners and Losers.* Brookfield, Conn.: Millbrook Press, 1995.

Jones, Norma. *Gambling: Who Wins?* Wylie, Texas: Information Plus, 1995.

Pascal, Francine. *Against the Odds (Sweet Valley High No. 51).* New York: Scholastic, 1989. Out of print, but may be available at libraries.

Savage, Jeff. *A Sure Thing: Sports and Gambling.* Minneapolis, Minn.: Lerner, 1997.

Booklets

Svendsen, Roger and Tom Griffin. *Gambling Choices and Guidelines,* Minnesota Dept. of Human Services and the Minnesota Institute of Public Health, 1997. Available free by calling 612-224-5121.

Svendsen, Roger. *Improving Your Odds: A Curriculum About Winning, Losing, and Staying Out of Trouble with Gambling.* Minnesota Dept. of Human Services and the Minnesota Institute of Public Health, 1997. To order, call 800-782-1878.

Wanna Bet: Everything You Ever Wanted to Know about Teen Gambling but Never Thought to Ask. Minnesota

Council on Compulsive Gambling, Inc., 1997. To order, call 218-722-1503 or write for more information to 314 West Superior Street, Suite 702, Duluth, MN 55802.

Medical Journal Articles

This is a list of recent articles about studies of teenage gambling that have been published in medical journals. The articles are written by medical experts, so they may be difficult to read, but may still be interesting to teens. The journals in which these articles appear are not usually available in school or public libraries. If you are interested in reading any of these articles, ask a librarian to help you obtain a copy of the article from a college or medical library. Librarians are glad to help students find this type of information.

Adebayo, B. "Gambling Behavior of Students in Grades Seven and Eight in Alberta, Canada." *Journal of School Health.* 68 (1998): 7–11. This study's surprising conclusion was that all students surveyed had gambled, either with lottery tickets, bingo, or sports betting.

Cunningham-Williams, R. M., Cottler, L. B., Compton, W. M. 3rd, et al. "Taking Chances: Problem Gamblers and Mental Health Disorders—Results from the St. Louis Epidemiologic Catchment Area Study. *American Journal of Public Health.* 88 (1998): 1093–1096. The study found that people who are being treated for psychiatric disorders often have problems with gambling.

Devlin, A. S., Peppard, D. M., Jr. "Casino Use by College Students." *Psychological Reports.* 78 (1996): 899–906. This study examined college students' gambling behavior at the Foxwoods Resort Casino in Connecticut.

Feigelman, W., Wallisch, L. S., Lesieur, H. R. "Problem Gamblers, Problem Substance Users, and Dual-Problem Individuals: An Epidemiological Study. *American Journal of Public Health.* 88 (1998): 467–470. This study found that young men who are problem gamblers are also likely to not be married, not to have a religious affiliation, and to have problems with the law.

Griffiths, M. D., Hunt, N. "Dependence on Computer Games by Adolescents." *Psychological Reports.* 82 (1998): 475–480. This study found that some teenagers can become addicted to playing computer games in the same way that people become addicted to gambling.

Kim, S. W. "Opioid Antagonists in the Treatment of Impulse-Control Disorders." *Journal of Clinical Psychiatry.* 59 (1998): 159–164. This study reviewed the effectiveness of using opioid antagonists, a type of medication, in treating compulsive gamblers.

Lopez, Viets V. C., Miller, W. R. "Treatment Approaches for Pathological Gamblers." *Clinical Psychology Review.* 17 (1997): 689–702. This study reviewed methods for teating pathological gambling, such as 12-step programs and behavioral therapy.

Pasternak, A. V. IV. "Pathologic Gambling: America's Newest Addiction?" *American Family Physician.* 56 (1997): 1293–1296. This article examines the role of the family physician in detecting and treating pathological gambling.

Phillips, D. P., Welty, W. R., Smith, M. M. "Elevated Suicide Levels Associated with Legalized Gambling." *Suicide Life-Threatening Behavior.* 27 (1997): 373–378. This study examined the suicide rates for cities where there is a lot of gambling, such as Atlantic City and Las Vegas, and found that these areas have higher suicide rates than other cities.

Proimos, J., DuRant, R. H., Pierce, J. D., et al. "Gambling and Other Risk Behaviors among 8th- to 12th-Grade Students." *Pediatrics.* 102 (1998): 23–30. This study found that teenagers who gamble are also likely to use alcohol, smoke cigarettes, avoid wearing a seatbelt, use inhalants, and carry a weapon.

Scotch, F. L., Fleger-Berman, L., Shaffer, H. J. "Evaluating he Impact of a Clinical Training Program in the Addictions." *Substance Use and Misuse.* 32 (1997): 1331–1348. This study examined how to help physicians learn more about problem gambling and other addictions and how to help teenagers recover from compulsive gambling.

Vitaro, F., Arseneault, L., Tremblay, R. E. "Dispositional Predictors of Problem Gambling in Male Adolescents." *American Journal of Psychiatry.* 154 (1997): 1769–1770. This study measured the lack of impulse control in teenage gamblers.

Wood, R. T. A., Griffiths, M.D. "The Acquisition, Development and Maintenance of Lottery and Scratchcard Gambling in Adolescence." *Journal of Adolescence.* 21 (1998): 265–273. This study examined the link between parental and child gambling, and found that many parents buy children lottery tickets.

INDEX

Page numbers in *italics* indicate illustrations.

111